George P. Delisser

Delisser's Horseman's Guide

George P. Delisser

Delisser's Horseman's Guide

ISBN/EAN: 9783337161156

Printed in Europe, USA, Canada, Australia, Japan

Cover: Foto ©Lupo / pixelio.de

More available books at **www.hansebooks.com**

DELISSER'S
HORSEMAN'S GUIDE.

COMPRISING

THE LAWS ON WARRANTY, AND THE RULES IN PURCHASING AND SELLING HORSES, WITH THE DECISIONS AND REPORTS OF VARIOUS COURTS IN EUROPE AND THE UNITED STATES.

TO WHICH IS ADDED

A DETAILED ACCOUNT OF WHAT CONSTITUTE SOUNDNESS AND UNSOUNDNESS, AND A PRECISE METHOD SIMPLY LAID DOWN, FOR THE EXAMINATION OF HORSES, SHOWING THEIR AGE TO THIRTY YEARS OLD.

TOGETHER WITH AN

EXPOSURE OF THE VARIOUS TRICKS AND IMPOSITIONS PRACTICED BY LOW HORSE DEALERS (JOCKEYS) ON INEXPERIENCED PERSONS.

ALSO

A valuable Table of each and every bone in the structure of the Horse.

THE ENTIRE MATTER CAREFULLY COMPILED FROM TWENTY ENGLISH, FIVE AMERICAN, SIX FRENCH, AND NINE GERMAN VETERINARY AUTHORS, WITH THE OPINIONS OF THE COMPILER ATTACHED.

BY

GEO. P. DELISSER, V. S. AND L. A.

And Late Examining Veterinary Surgeon to the American Society for the Prevention of Cruelty to Animals.

NEW YORK:
DICK & FITZGERALD, PUBLISHERS,
18 ANN STREET.

Entered according to Act of Congress, in the year 1875, by

DICK & FITZGERALD,

In the Office of the Librarian of Congress, at Washington, D. C.

PREFACE.

The leading object of this work is to present to the public, in a handy form for the pocket, a detailed enumeration of the various diseases and infirmities which constitute unsoundness in horses, with plain directions for detecting them, even when concealment has been attempted by such dealers as are more ingenious than honest.

There are quite a number of persons who consider themselves well informed in regard to the legal enactments relating to unsoundness, by which the rights of purchasers are defended against fraudulent horse-dealers; there are, however, comparatively few who might not become easy victims in a horse trade, notwithstanding their supposed knowledge. For their benefit, and for the guidance also of those who lay no claim to any knowledge on the subject, the laws which regulate horse transactions are laid down, together with such legal decisions as bear on doubtful points; thus affording a reliable book of reference useful to all, whether buyer or seller, lawyer or client.

Among the other subjects introduced may be mentioned the most reliable methods of discovering the correct age of a horse; the points by which a good, sound horse may be known; the most desirable and appropriate food, and various other useful information connected with the general management of horses.

The author has taken special pains to condense into an apparently small space as much plain information and instruction as possible, omitting nothing that is necessary to render each topic complete and comprehensible, but excluding all needless repetitions and tedious explanations, as calculated to detract from the main objects of the work—perspicuity, accuracy and ready reference.

CONTENTS.

	PAGE.
ON SOUNDNESS	7
IN WHAT SOUNDNESS CONSISTS	7, 10
WHAT CONSTITUTES UNSOUNDNESS	8
LEGAL AND OTHER DECISIONS	8, 10, 11, 20
PROSPECTIVE UNSOUNDNESS	15
DISEASES WHICH PRODUCE UNSOUNDNESS	21, 33
BLEMISHES	33
ON WARRANTY	34
FORM OF WARRANTY	34
BREACH OF WARRANTY	35
LEGAL AND OTHER DECISIONS	37, 40
DIFFERENT KINDS OF WARRANTIES	41
ADVICE TO BUYERS	47
HINTS ON EXAMINING HORSES	49
HOW TO DETECT LAMENESS	50
THE SOLE OF THE FOOT	51
DEFECTS OF THE HOOF, &C	52
THE LEGS	54
THE EYE	55
THE WIND	58
HOW TO DETECT CHRONIC COUGH	60
ROARING	61
THE KIDNEYS	62
VICIOUS HABITS	63

CONTENTS.

	PAGE
TRICKS OF HORSE-DEALERS	64
ARTIFICIAL MARKS	66
RECEIPTS FOR COLORING	66

ON AGE AND APPEARANCE 67

THE NUMBER OF TEETH	67
THE STRUCTURE OF THE TEETH	68
THE AGE TOLD BY THE TEETH	69
THE AGE TOLD BY THE EYES	71
THE AGE TOLD BY THE CHIN	73
THE AGE TOLD BY THE LOWER JAW BONE	74
THE RACE HORSE	82
DRIVING	83

ON FEEDING, AND THE FOOD 83

COMPARATIVE TABLE OF FOOD	87
DIRECTIONS FOR FEEDING	87

TABLE OF THE BONES IN A HORSE 89

THE HORSEMAN'S GUIDE.

ON SOUNDNESS.

Under this heading we propose to treat on Soundness and Unsoundness, and give a clear explanation of the legal interpretations on the subject.

In what does Soundness consist? According to Mr. Spooner,—"This question has been a subject of the most contradictory opinions, has given birth to numerous arguments, and has sadly puzzled the heads of lawyers themselves. Indeed, the most opposite opinions have been expressed by the learned judges at various times; though, at the present day, when the opinion of veterinary surgeons are allowed more weight than formerly, the decisions of the bench are much more uniform. Perfect soundness appears to consist of the total absence of disease; but as this very seldom occurs in horses that have been used, and as, from the rarity of its existence, the strict definition would be useless, it is now understood to mean that a horse has no disease or alteration of structure that makes him in any respect less useful, or is likely to make him less useful, than he would be without such defect. Soundness has, therefore, strict reference to utility; it does not apply to blemishes, although these blemishes may be alterations of structure, and produced by disease. Freedom from blemishes must be specified in the warranty, in order to guard against them. With regard to the greater number of points, veterinary surgeons are pretty well agreed as to what is unsoundness and what is not; but there are cases in which there is a difference of opinion; some practitioners, perhaps, are too strict in their opinions, and others not strict enough, but there are many, it is to be hoped, who preserve the happy medium."

Mr. Youatt says,—"The horse is unsound that labors under disease, or has some alteration of structure which does interfere, or is likely to interfere, with his natural usefulness. The term *natural usefulness* must be borne in mind, as it has received high judicial sanction. *Coates vs. Stephens*, 2 Moody and Robinson, 157; *Scholefield vs. Robb*, ibid. 210. The following extract is taken from a note to one of those cases: '*As it may now be considered as settled law, that the breach of a warranty or soundness does not entitle the purchaser to return the horse, but only to recover the difference of value of the horse, with or without the particular unsoundness, the question of temporary maladies, producing no permanent deterioration of the animal, would, generally speaking, only involve a right to damages merely nominal.*' Therefore natural usefulness has been decided on, as one horse may possess great speed, but soon is knocked up; another will work all day, but cannot be got beyond a snail's pace; a third with a heavy tread is liable to stumble, and is continually putting to hazard the neck of his rider; another, with an irritable constitution, and a loose, washy form, loses his appetite and begins to scour if a little extra work is exacted from him. The term unsoundness must *not* be applied to either of these; it would be opening far too widely a door to disputation and endless wrangling. The buyer can discern, or ought to know, whether the form of the horse is that which will render him likely to suit his purpose, and he should try him sufficiently to ascertain his natural strength, endurance, and manner of going. Unsoundness, we repeat, has reference only to disease, or to that alteration of structure which is connected with, or will produce disease, and lessen the usefulness of the animal."

In "Hippopathology," I find Mr. Percival saying,—"Reluctantly as we enter on this difficult and much debated question, we feel it our duty, in a work on lameness, to make some observations on the subject, though these observations will be rather of a general, than of a particular nature, and have special reference to soundness regarded as the converse of or opposite state to lameness. No person buys or sells a horse without feeling some concern as to the soundness of the animal; the purchaser is apprehensive lest his new horse should from any cause turn out unserviceable, or unequal to that for the performance of which he has bought him; the vender is apprehensive, either lest the animal, in other hands, should not prove that sound and effective servant he conceived or represented him to be, or lest some unrepresented or concealed fault or defect, he is aware the animal possesses, may now, in his new master's hands, be brought to light. Soundness, as opposed to actual or decided lameness (or as synonymous with good health), is a state too well understood to need any definition or description: when we come, however, to draw a line between soundness and lameness in their less distinguishable forms—to mark the point at which one ends and the other begins—we meet a difficulty; and this difficulty increases when we find ourselves called on to include under our denomination of unsoundness, that which is likely, or has a tendency to bring forth lameness.

The number of 'horse cases,' as they are commonly called, that have engaged the attention of our courts of law, have brought eminent persons of the legal profession to our aid in the solution of this intricate question. Lord Mansfield, years ago, made an attempt to settle the point according to an *ad valorem* scale; setting every horse down as sound in the eye of the law, whose value or cost amounted to a certain sum. This, of course, was law that never could hold in horse transactions.

Lord Ellenborough legislated with a great deal more knowledge of horse-flesh.

The law he laid down was, that *any infirmity* which rendered a horse less *fit* for present use or convenience, constituted unsoundness—a law which, though it admitted of great latitude of construction, and to some special cases did not prove applicable at all, was still a wholesome and practicable one in a majority of cases of dispute.

Lord Tenterden made but little improvement on it, when he pronounced every horse unsound that could not go through the same labor as before the existence of the defect or blemish in dispute, and with the same degrees of facility.

Professor Coleman's notion was that every horse ought to be considered sound that could perform the ordinary duties of an ordinary horse. This definition is open to the same objections as the judicial laws of Lords Mansfield and Tenterden. Mange, diseases of the eye (so long as they are confined to one eye,) nay, glanders, and farcy even, in certain stages, and some other diseases, do not incapacitate a horse, and yet they all amount to palpable unsoundness. On the other hand, many a horse, from age or want of condition, or from possessing a constitution naturally weak or washy, is unfitted for what might be considered the ordinary duties of an ordinary horse, and yet cannot be called *unsound*. Then, again, comes for explanation, what are to be regarded as the *ordinary duties*, and what we are to look upon as an *ordinary horse?* both presumptions equally indefinable with Lord Ellenborough's standard of *fitness*, and Lord Tenterden's *status quo* before the existence of the defect or blemish.

The late Mr. Castley, veterinary surgeon to the 12th Lancers—whose opinions on this subject, as well as on every other, his habits of acute and accurate observation rendered of peculiar value to us—felt inclined, to use his own words, "to steer a middle course," in accordance with which he ventured on the following propositions: First, *That all recognized disease constitutes unsoundness for the time being.* Secondly, That changes of structure, or an altered condition of parts, and derangement or impairment of function, are allowed by all to be our two great landmarks in conducting examinations for soundness. The first of these propositions may fairly be included in the second; all disease consisting either in change of structure or change of function, and most diseases involving both these changes. And in regard to the second rule for our guidance, obvious and decisive as are changes of structure, combined with deranged or impaired function of parts in general, there are still some of that trifling or uninfluential nature that can hardly, when they do exist, be looked upon as unsoundness; such are chronic or partial diseases of certain parts or organs, the obliteration of a vein or artery, for example, the conversion of fibro-cartilage into bone, as in splint, chronic or partial disease of such an organ as the liver, etc., etc."

Our present inquiry into the nature of soundness being restricted to its relation to *lameness*, and it being our intention here to deal with broad principles, leaving the nicer shades of distinction for consideration until such time as we come to treat of particular lameness, we may safely say that every horse showing lameness must be pronounced unsound; although the converse of this, as a fundamental principle, will by no means hold good—every horse *not* showing lameness not necessarily being (considered as) a sound horse. For instance, a horse may have a spavin, or a curb, or a swollen back sinew, and still evince no lameness, even though he may show marks of having been fired or blistered for the same, and so give us every reason to believe that formerly he has experienced actual lameness from one or other of these defects. Would, however, any veterinary surgeon, under these circumstances, give a certificate of soundness? If he did, it must be qualified in a manner that would little induce any person to purchase such a horse, unless at a price consonant with the evident reduction of its value. It will be requisite, therefore, for us to say, not simply that every *lame* horse is unsound, but to add the words, *or that has that about him which is likely on work to render him lame.* This will, it is true, open the door to difference of opinion and equivocation. There may, as we have seen, spring up two opinions concerning the presence even of lameness. There will in more cases be two opinions concerning that which is accounted to be the precursor of lameness, or have a tendency at some period, proximate or remote, to produce lameness; all which differences are best got rid of by reference to the ablest veterinary advice. There will be less diversity of opinion among professional men than among others, and the more *skillful* and *respectable* the professional persons are, the greater will be the probability of a happy unison in their views of the case. To lay down

ON SOUNDNESS. 13

any *statute law* which shall meet such cases as these, is, from the very nature of vital structures and functions, totally an impossible matter.

We ought to be able to establish it as an axiom, although it may prove one not unassailable by argument, *that a lame horse is an unsound horse.* It might be objected, for example, that a horse having a stone in his foot—(than which nothing, for the time, renders a horse more lame)—should be regarded as unsound; and yet by this rule he must be so considered as long as he continues lame, though as sound from the moment that the stone is removed. The shoe, nailed on too tight, furnishes another similar example. A horse, quite sound, enters a forge to be shod, and comes out going, as grooms call it, *scrambling, i. e.*, lame; he is, in fact, no longer a sound horse; take him back, however, into the forge, and remove his shoes, nail them on easy, and, if not completely restored to soundness, he is thereby evidently so much relieved as to give pretty fair earnest of his becoming well, or as sound as ever, by the next or the following day. It may be said, and we quite agree in the reply, that such trivial points as these are not likely to come before us for decision, or to cause us any trouble if they do; still it is right we should be armed on all sides to defend that law which we, as professional men, deem it wholesome and just to lay down; viz.: *That every horse going lame (no matter from what cause) ought to be pronounced unsound.*

If any real objection can be urged to the institution of such a law, one presents itself in the case of a horse that is lame at one time and sound at another; for instance, a horse may have a frush, or thrush, of which he shall flinch, or go palpably lame every time he happens to tread upon a stone, or whenever he goes upon hard, uneven surfaces, though at other times, upon soft ground, or upon turf, he will appear quite sound. This horse, we think, stands, in respect to the question of soundness, altogether in a different position from either the stone-in-the-foot or the tight-shoe case: here is *disease*—demonstrable disease; and although it gives rise but occasionally to lameness, still, as lameness is at times the result, we hold that the horse ought to be accounted unsound. The *spavin*—in certain forms—affords another example of temporary or transitory lameness; a spavined horse may come excessively lame out of his stable in the morning, but after having gone a while and waxed warm, will no longer exhibit lameness or even stiffness of his hock. In accordance with the laws of the judges, and with that of our late Professor (Coleman), such a horse being *not* less fit for present use or convenience, being able to go through the same labor as before the defect or blemish, able to perform the ordinary duties of an ordinary horse—such a horse, we repeat, must be pronounced, so long as he continues in this aptitude, to be sound; whereas, however much we may differ concerning other points, we believe all veterinarians will concur with us in the opinion in declaring the occasionally lame spavined—if not the lame frushed—horse to be unsound, notwithstanding his redeeming quality of becoming sound on work, and of continuing so to the end of that work.

However strong we may feel ourselves in our axiom, that a lame horse must be accounted unsound, the moment, as we observed before, we attempt the converse of it—viz., that every horse free from lameness is (as respects the question of lameness) to be held as sound, we change into a position most infirm and untenable. All sorts of diseases and defects stare us in the face, which, though not the immediate producers of lameness, too surely, in our minds,

ON SOUNDNESS. 15

betoken its approach, waiting only for work or other exciting cause for its development; and with such betokenment before us it is quite impossible we can, with any show of reason or equity, pronounce the horse having them, notwithstanding he at the time goes free from lameness, to be virtually a sound horse; for how can we in conscience call that horse sound that we know has that about him which will probably—nay, certainly, cause him to become lame the first long or heavy day's work he is put to perform? As well might we call an apple or a pear sound which we know to be rotten at the core; and yet, strictly and literally speaking, the animal goes *sound*—is as sound in *action*, to *appearance*, as is the rotten apple or pear. In cases where so much difficulty—nay, impossibility, presents itself to the drawing of a distinction between the two opposite, and (as we may call them) abhorrent states of soundness and unsoundness, it has struck us some good might arise from a division of *unsoundness* into *actual* and *prospective*, the latter denomination indicating a state of *transient* or *trustless* soundness.

Notwithstanding a horse may be free from lameness, may go sound, yet, so long as he has that about him which will probably or surely render him lame the first time he is put to hard work, he is *virtually* an unsound horse, in honesty unwarrantable; and the best denomination we are able to find for such a failable condition—a sort of intermediate state between soundness and unsoundness—is *prospective unsoundness*. So far as abstract action is concerned, the horse, it is true, must be regarded as sound, although that which he has upon him, making him liable or certain to become lame whenever he is put to excess of action or work, certainly stands in the way of any warranty of soundness being given.

PROSPECTIVE unsoundness, however, although it relieves us from the necessity of doing that which no professional man conscientiously can do in very many of the subjects brought before him—viz., of pronouncing the horse either actually sound or unsound—yet unfortunately it opens a door through which crowds of cases, really doubtful in their character or rendered so by the variety of opinions given on them, are ready to be forced in, and made to perplex us in coming to any proper or judicious selection of them. One horse has manifest *disease*, in some form or another, as the cause of his being pronounced likely or certain to go lame at no very remote period; his case admits of no question. But another horse has no disease, only a *malformation*, a *deformity*, or *misshapenness*, the result of which is weakness of limb and consequent liability to failure—to lameness, in fact. A third horse has neither disease nor deformity, nothing but a bad habit, and that is said to amount to unsoundness; and it is the cases that come under one or other of these latter denominations—which are the offspring either of natural defect, of use or wear, or of habit—that, for the most part, puzzle veterinary practitioners in coming to judicious decisions on soundness.

To elucidate these observations by example: A horse may have a spavin or a curb, or a swollen or fired back sinew—any disease, in short, from which, on exertion, he is likely, as our experience tells us, to become lame; such a horse is *prospectively* unsound. But suppose he have a club foot, a parrot mouth, bent limbs, curved or curly-looking hocks, narrow or flat feet, weak joints, a hip down, etc.—all natural deformities or malformations, none of them coming fairly or popularly under the category of disease—what is to be done in passing judgment upon them? The equitable adjudication appears to be, as in the case of disease, to declare that any of them constitutes unsoundness that is probable or certain to give rise, on work, to lameness; but then we shall experience difficulty, in some of the cases, in drawing the line between actual lameness and natural failing or weakness. A horse foaled with evident deficiency of physical power, partial or general, can hardly be called unsound; though should he have that about him which renders it likely he will, when put to work, become *actually* lame, he ought, assuredly, be pronounced *prospectively* so. *Cutting* (as striking one foot against its fellow leg is called), arise from whatever cause it may, is apt to produce occasional lameness, and when it does so is fairly regarded as a species of prospective unsoundness. *Springhalt* is action so unnatural that some do not hesitate to affirm it to be a species of unsoundness, though it is a well-known fact that many horses so affected will do the same amount of work as it is reasonable to suppose they would or could do were they free from it. After all, as the foregoing observations will abundantly testify, a good deal in the decisions between soundness and unsoundness must be left to the skill and judgment of the professional man; he alone can unriddle the true nature of the case, and form a just estimate of the probabilities of lameness; and if he be but trustworthy and honest in his opinions, he is, beyond question, the preferable authority in such cases of appeal for advice.

When we, as men acquainted with the animal economy, consider the multiplicity of evils even quadruped flesh is heir to, and reflect in how many ways its health and action may become impaired, and how graduated down those impairments may be into states of indisputable soundness, we have no right to feel surprised at the intricacy in which we find the subject before us involved, no more than we have, in a strictly pathological point of view, at the comparative paucity of sound horses coming under our observation. The separation of monomania in man from oddity or eccentricity is hardly more difficult than resolving the question of soundness in its dubious or transitory form is in horses; a great deal, after all, must be matter of opinion, and those opinions will ever prove best worthy our reliance which are founded on the widest experience, coupled with the best character for honesty.

No more responsible duty attaches to a professional man than that of giving a *certificate of soundness**: by it the warranty of the dealer or vender is either confirmed or falsified, the purchase completed or set on one side, the value of the animal either established or destroyed; on all which accounts the veterinarian is pledged, not only to use his hundred eyes in making the examination, but also his maturest judgment in diving into the nature of any unsoundness he may discover, as well as into its positive or probable effect on the action or capabilities of the animal, both present and to come. This leads us, before we close the subject, to inform our readers, that unless a certificate of soundness or unsoundness be obtained from qualified and actual professional men, it ought not to be of any value, not only from their want of knowledge, but in those cases you will find that the more ignorant the quack is, the more he will imagine himself capable; besides, those men, as you will find, overrun almost every city in the United States, put on appearance, such as stylish dress, and drive a dashing wagon and pair; all this is done to deceive and attract the public—a sort of advertisement—thinking, that as he

---

* As the United States are so overrun with quacks and impostors personating themselves as Veterinary Surgeons, certificates on soundness and unsoundness can be obtained from such men by purchase, *i. e.*, bribe.

cannot merit talent, he may merit appearance, and by that, cause the public to think more of him. To further acquaint our readers, and caution them against placing any value on certificates obtained from quacks and such class of men, we shall here give a case that took place in Brooklyn, New York. A bay mare seven years old was sold to a butcher for $250.00, by a sale stable keeper, and warranted sound, kind, and true in all harness. The butcher took him right away to a man (calling himself a veterinary surgeon, and doing a first-class business, driving a dashing team), for examining. This quack pronounced the mare *unsound*, and obtained $5.00. On the sale stable keeper hearing this, he started off to the man who examined the mare, and asked him how could he do such a thing, as it will injure him?—to pass the mare as sound and he will give him $20.00. The quack said, as an excuse, I will examine her again, which he did, and passed her as *sound;* this I can vouch for, having heard it from the sale stable keeper, as well as from the butcher; and I was shown the mare some time afterwards, and found that she was unsound, having a spavin of the off leg, and lame. This will inform our readers of the value of certificates obtained from such class of men.

I shall make a few remarks regarding the soundness and unsoundness in cases of pulmonary disease, as cases are recorded of horses being sold as sound, and in a day or two the animal showed signs of pneumonia or pleurisy, and the animal died within eight or ten days from the date of purchase. The purchaser, in such a case, contends that the horse must have been diseased at the time of purchase, and not sound, as represented on the warranty; but in such an opinion the purchaser is greatly mistaken, as a horse might be sound on the day of sale, but the removal of the animal to another stable, the exposure of the animal to the wind or damp air, may produce a pulmonary disease, and prove fatal within two to ten days. To justify me in that opinion, I shall quote from Mr. Percival, (in Lecture xxxviii, p. 323,) who says: "Pulmonary disease runs its course now and then with surprising rapidity. I have known a horse to be attacked with acute pneumonia, and to die from it in the space of seventeen hours; and it is by no means uncommon for it to prove fatal on the second or third day from its onset. Ignorance of this fact has led to the institution of many lawsuits, and to some *oppressive judicial arbitrations* for horse-dealers; *e. g.*, a gentleman purchases a young horse, warranted sound, and the next day, or the day after, rides or drives the animal, unprepared for fatigue, and consequently unable to bear it, by way of trial; the day following this trial, or rather ordeal, the horse refuses his food, blows a little, and soon after manifests a severe attack of pneumonia, of which, within a few days or weeks from his purchase, he dies. An action is immediately brought against the dealer; some blundering, ignorant farrier, on the part of the plaintiff, swears that the animal, when opened, was found as *rotten as a pear*, and that *he must consequently have been diseased long before he was bought.* The result is that the dealer is cast, and the gentleman recovers his money; now, in the generality of these cases, the very reverse of this is the absolute truth; the animal was perfectly sound at the time of purchase, and was made otherwise solely by the exertion his purchaser put him to; and so far from the *rottenness of the lungs,* or agglutination of them to the sides of the chest, being proofs of the contrary, I have seen the one produced in seventeen hours, and know, from extensive observation, that the other, viz., blackness and engorgement of them with blood, or something like an approach to mortification (for rottenness is an expression that has here no definite meaning whatever), may take place in the course of four-and-twenty hours. Indeed, when pneumonia proves fatal, it most commonly does so in the course of the first three, or four, or five days; if it continue beyond this, or there be any remission, it is always a favorable indication. In these cases, the lungs themselves, as I have just stated, are found nearly black, of the color of the darkest venous blood, with which they are prodigiously glutted; the pleura also displays a surface highly vascular, and adhesions are occasionally discovered upon it.

I shall now give a list of the various diseases and infirmities that are usually supposed to cause unsoundness, viz.:

BROKEN KNEES are considered as unsoundness, while the wound is open, or from an enlargement caused thereby, or from the wound being of such a nature as to interfere with the action of the joint, or where the horse goes lame from the injury.

CAPPED HOCKS are considered as unsoundness, as the difficulty of ascertaining whether the enlargement was caused from merely lying on uneven flooring, from a sprain, or from latent injury of the hock, causes the decision to be given in such a manner as to guard against future troubles, and to protect the purchaser from having a crippled horse, after supposing him to be a sound one.

CONTRACTION is considered as unsoundness *only* when considerable heat is felt at the posterior portion of the foot, where the frog is diseased, or when lameness is present.

CORNS are considered as unsoundness when they are of a size as to, in all probability, cause the horse to be lame at some future time, or if he is lame at the time.

COUGH is considered as unsoundness, no matter how

slight or trivial, as it can run on to some fatal pulmonary disease, and in many cases become of a chronic nature, which will, in some degree, impair the health of the animal, and render him far less able to perform the same work than he would be if the chronic cough was not present.

CATARACT and other alterations of the structure in the eyes, that impede, or are likely to impede vision, are to be considered as unsoundness.

CRIB-BITING is considered as unsoundness; as, though at first but a vicious habit, its ultimate effect is to injure both strength and condition, besides the occasional breaking or wearing of the front teeth, making the animal old before his time, and sometimes rendering it difficult or impossible for him to graze, when it is absolutely necessary for the benefit of the animal that he should be turned out to grass.

CURBS are considered as unsoundness, (unless the horse has worked with them for many months without injury or inconvenience,) or should there be inflammation or tenderness of the parts, or the animal lame. A horse is not returnable if he starts a curb in five minutes after the purchase, as it can be done in a moment, and does not necessarily indicate any previous unsoundness, or weakness of the part.

CUTTING is considered as unsoundness, as it is liable to render the animal seriously injured by its oft-repeated striking; it thickens the parts and enlarges the fetlock, and very often the entire leg is swollen to a great extent; it is also indicative that he is either weak, or has an awkwardness of gait inconsistent with safety, which may be deemed a serious imperfection. Cutting on the inside, immediately below the knee joint, called *speedy cut*, is also a material defect, as it sometimes causes the horse to fall suddenly in trotting or galloping, and in many instances interferes with the action of the knee joint, and renders the animal seriously crippled.

COLD is considered as unsoundness while the animal is suffering from it as, however slight the cold may be, it is difficult to ascertain if it may not be the forerunner of some serious cerebral or pulmonary disease; if the cold be chronic, then it is actual unsoundness, as it interferes with the health of the animal, and causes him to be much weaker, and liable to exhaustion when given extra work.

ENLARGED GLANDS are considered unsoundness; if the engorgement under the jaw is of a large size, tender to the touch, and if the gland at the root of the ear partakes of the enlargement, and the membrane of the nose is redder than it should be, we must then look on those signs as a symptom of disease.

ENLARGED HOCK is considered as unsoundness, as it is generally caused from strains; and, as this joint is a complicated one, it will be materially affected by a strain, although the probability may be that the horse will stand work without lameness; there is absolutely a weakness of the part, and a possibility of lameness at any moment after a hard day's work.

There is an enlargement of the hock, caused by kicks or blows, or other external injuries, which must not be mistaken for one caused from strains, as one is merely an enlargement of the skin, or immediately under it, or on the outside of the bone, while the other is a strain of the ligaments which confine the small bones of the hock; the one caused from some external injury may be designated as a blemish only.

EYES AFFECTED are to be considered as unsoundness so long as the eyes are at all affected, no matter how slightly, as, this organ being of such a delicate nature, any disease of the eye may terminate in blindness; a slight cold may so weaken the eyes that a local inflammation may arise, from which it may run on to an obstinate case of ophthalmia, then to a cataract, and finally blindness.

ENLARGEMENT OF THE SINEWS OR LIGAMENTS is to be considered as unsoundness, as it is caused from severe strain, not only so that the tendons are inflamed, but often trouble arises from effusion of blood in the sheath, and the disease, whether trivial or severe, should never be thought lightly of, as it in all probability may render the animal a cripple; lameness may not be present, but such a horse is to be looked on as in duty bound to go lame at any moment, and is in all cases an unsound one.

FOUNDER is considered as unsoundness, whether in the acute or chronic form; as the elasticity of the laminæ is somewhat destroyed, and the foot generally assumes an utterly unnatural shape, if not in the external appearance, most invariably in the internal portion of the foot. When the disease has been going on for some time, the elastic substances between the laminæ and the pedal bone, as well as the fine horny lamellæ between them and the crust, lose the property of extension, and the horn of the crust is secreted by nature of a more spongy character, and much thicker in substance, than in health; the sole is always flatter than natural, and causes in many instances the convex sole; besides, from the nature of the disease, the muscles of the chest generally waste away from want of proper action, caused by the attitude of the animal during the disease; no matter how well the animal might appear after an attack of founder (Laminitis) no person can give a warranty on such a horse, as he is liable at any time, from the slightest chill, or other slight causes, to be attacked again. In fact, he is actually susceptible to the disease, having once had it, and lameness might appear at any moment.

FARCY constitutes unsoundness, no matter if the disease has been made to entirely disappear, and the animal appear in perfect health; as farcy is a disease of the absorbents, it is not only a difficult matter, but almost impossible, to thoroughly eradicate the poison from the system, and the animal might be attacked with it at any time, with scarcely any premonitory symptoms, and die in a very short period after the second attack.

GLANDERS constitutes unsoundness (*see Farcy*), as the two diseases are similar in their nature, only differing in the mode of attack, and all said on farcy is applicable to glanders.

GUTTA SERENA constitutes unsoundness, although the eyes appear natural to an ordinary observer; yet, if but one eye is affected, it is an unsound horse.

LAMENESS constitutes unsoundness, no matter from what cause, however temporary it may be, or obscure, there must be disease or alteration of structure, which must lessen the usefulness of the animal, and render him unsound for the time. Lord Ellenborough says, "I have always held, and now hold, that a warranty of soundness is broken, if the animal, at the time of sale, has an infirmity upon him which renders him less fit for present service." It is not necessary that the disorder should be permanent or incurable. The horse in question having been lame at the time of sale, when he was warranted to be sound, his condition subsequently is no defense to the action; see 4 *Campbell* 251, *Elton vs. Brogden.* Mr. Baron Parke confirms this doctrine; for while a horse is lame, it would really be not only contrary to common sense, but conflicting with the English language, to say that he was sound; besides, the actual custom, and decisions by various courts, regards a lame horse as an unsound one.

Megrims are considered unsoundness, for under this somewhat obscure name we have vertigo, apoplexy, convulsions from various causes, etc.; but no matter what may be the actual nature of the disease, as megrims, it is an unsoundness, as it is a disease, whether it be caused from a fullness of the blood-vessels of the brain, or by water in its ventricles or cavities, or from a rupture of a small blood-vessel—they are all dangerous in their action, and a horse once attacked is predisposed to a second, a third, and repeated attacks, endangering the life of his driver the entire time he is being used, and, as Mr. Youatt says: "That a horse that has had a second attack is never to be trusted."

Neurotomy is to be considered as unsoundness, as unsoundness by us means any defect in (or absence of) any vital portion of the animal's structure, so as to render him liable at any time to suffer from the want of it, unless an argument can be established that nature gave the nerve for no use whatever, which could not be very well done. A horse may stand work well after the operation, but from the want of that nervous influence, various troubles might arise, and render the animal unfit for use. Chief-Justice Best held that a horse having had the operation of neurotomy performed on him, is an unsound horse; and Mr. Youatt says, in his opinion, there cannot be any doubt about the matter.

Ossification of the lateral cartilages is considered as unsoundness, as it interferes with the natural expansion of the foot, and in horses of quick work, almost universally produces lameness. Says Mr. Youatt, this is absolutely a serious disease, involving, in many instances, the pedal bone. It is caused by concussion, and renders the animal sore and travel-short a day after he has had any work, especially over hard and rugged streets.

PUMICED FOOT is considered unsoundness when the union between the horny and sensible laminæ, or little plates of the foot, is weakened, and the coffin-bone is let down and presses upon the sole; "when the sole yields to this unnatural weight, and becomes rounded, and is brought in contact with the ground, and is bruised and injured, that horse must be unsound, and unsound forever, because there are no means by which we can raise the coffin-bone again into its place," says Mr. Youatt.

PARALYSIS is to be considered as unsoundness, as it is a disorganization of some part of the nervous system, and must be considered as such ; although great difficulty may arise to trace it to its seat, yet sufficient is known of the disease to designate it as an unsoundness. Various causes might be the means of bringing on this trouble, but no matter the cause, the result is what we are to deal with; an animal having been once affected, is very much predisposed to a future attack, besides the actual weakness that must remain for some time at the spot where the disease was seated ; and the *only* manner in which a horse that has had paralysis could be warranted, is, after the animal has been worked as an ordinary horse, and for a time not less than twelve months, without showing any signs of its return.

QUITTOR is to be considered as unsoundness, (no matter if the abscess ceases to discharge its humor and the wound healed,) should any enlargement of the coronet remain, or the foot in any manner altered in its size or shape from its fellow ; for if an enlargement remain, we might be certain that the cartilages have been affected ; and if the foot be in any way altered in its structure, we may also come to the conclusion that some of the bones of the foot, as well as the cartilages, are affected, and the animal liable to go lame at any moment.

QUIDDING is an unsoundness when confirmed, and cannot be stopped by various means; for instance, quidding might be caused from a sore mouth, and after the sore is healed he ceases to quid; also, from sharp edges of his teeth, or from irregularity of them, which could be remedied by filing off the edges, or filing off, or extracting the teeth or tooth that causes the irregularity, and he will cease to quid. But if he quids from none of the causes named, or from any cause that cannot be treated so as to remove the continuance of the habit, then it is unsoundness, as it materially impairs the usefulness of the animal, and his constitution so affected as to make him almost a living skeleton, as in many instances a morbid state of the pharynx is induced by giving balls improperly, which renders deglutition difficult, and sometimes impossible. Mr. Armatage says, "Sometimes there is a partial palsy of the muscles employed in deglutition, by which the animal has been gradually starved; therefore such a termination to any disease, or vice, or whatever it may be termed, must be considered as unsoundness."

RINGBONE is to be considered as unsoundness, no matter how small the tumor may be, or the animal traveling without showing any signs of lameness; the situation of this disease is such, that, from the action of the foot, and the stress upon the part, the inflammation and the formation of bone may acquire a tendency to spread so rapidly, that we must pronounce the slightest enlargement of the pasterns, or around the coronet, to be unsoundness; according to Mr. Youatt, it is somewhat similar to ossification of the lateral cartilages.

ON SOUNDNESS.

RHEUMATISM is to be considered as unsoundness, as, in most instances, an animal once attacked is predisposed to it again on the slightest cause, and very often the attack is periodical. Chronic rheumatism of the muscles is more lasting than the acute, as during its slow process, it often flies from one part to another, attacking the ligaments and tendons, as well as the muscular fibres; it is seldom much under control, and the animal's general health suffers, but a horse attacked with rheumatism after he comes into the hand of the purchaser is not returnable, unless the purchaser can prove that he was so attacked previously.

ROARING, BROKEN-WIND, THICK-WIND, are to be considered as unsoundness, as it is a disease of some of the muscles whose office is to dilate the larynx; they are somewhat wasted away and flabby (crico-arytenoidens lateralis and thyro-arytenoidens) and other muscles are no doubt equally atrophied. The causes of roaring are said to be of three kinds by Mr. Walsh. "First, inflammation, which has left a thickening or ulceration of the mucous membrane, or a fungous growth from it; secondly, paralysis of the muscle; and thirdly, an alteration of the shape of the cartilages of the larynx, produced by tight reining. Therefore, a horse whose mode of breathing is not only disagreeable to his driver, but injurious to himself, is unsound; as it is caused from disease, and must impair that portion of the muscles so affected as to be of some vital injury to the animal, should he ever be attacked with any pulmonary disease.

The other two diseases named are similar to unsoundness, they being only modifications of roaring.

SAND-CRACK, QUARTER-CRACK, is to be considered as unsoundness. Mr. Youatt says, "It may, however, occur without the slightest warning, and no horse can be rejected on account of sand-crack that has been sprung after purchase." A horse may travel well, but as he is likely to be lame at any time, and seriously so, it renders him an unsound horse.

Spavin-Bone is an unsoundness, unless the animal has had it on him for years, and showed no lameness during that time. To give the reader an idea, we would say that if a horse nine years old or thereabouts, has a spavin, and goes well, showing no signs of lameness on taking him from his stall after some rest, and proof is given that he has had that enlargement on him for two or three years, he is not an unsound horse; but if a young horse of four to six years old have on him a spavin, and it has been there but a few months, even if he is not lame, he can never be passed as a sound horse, as it is probable that on the bony deposit extending itself over the joint of the hock, the small bones, or even the larger ones, may become affected as to render him lame for life; therefore, the motto for bone-spavin is, "Consider him unsound until time has proved him otherwise."

Spavin-Bog or Blood is to be considered as unsoundness when there is any lameness present, no matter how slight, or if much heat is felt at the parts, as Mr. Youatt says, "he considers it as an unsoundness, because, although it may not be productive of lameness at slow work, the rapid and powerful action of the hock in quicker motion will produce *permanent*, yet perhaps not considerable lameness, which can scarcely ever be with certainty removed."

Mr. Spooner says: "Blood-spavin is certainly unsoundness, unless extremely slight, although in the majority of cases it does not cause lameness."

Mr. Armatage says: "If bog-spavin be very slight, and unattended with stiffness, I do not consider them as unsoundness; if, however, they are considerable, or attended with the slightest stiffness, they must be considered as such."

SPLINT is to be considered as unsoundness, if, according to its situation, likely to affect the action of a joint, or to press upon any tendon or ligament; or if recent, and evincing tenderness on being pressed; or if they are so large as to be struck by the other leg; but if they are small or moderate in size, and have existed for some time without occasioning lameness, then the animal may be considered as sound, provided the animal is about eight or nine years old; but in a young horse, of about five or six years old, it should be guarded against by a sufficient warranty, though no lameness be present.

SPEEDY CUT is to be considered as unsoundness, as the probability is that it has been caused by striking the other leg, just below the knee-joint, with the other foot, which is generally the result of high-action horses; and the possibility of its extending so near to the knee-joint as to interfere with its action, as the horse is so much more likely to continue striking the part after it is enlarged than previously, and if he did before the enlargement was present, he must strike it now more severely, and keep up an incessant irritation, which must eventually lame the animal; the use of the knee-boot does not in any way lessen the disease—it may only be the means of keeping off his lameness to a later date; and the only case where he can be passed as a sound horse is when (as in splint or spavin) he has had it on him for some time, without occasioning lameness, and is of an advanced age; otherwise he is unsound.

STRINGHALT is to be considered as unsoundness, as it is incurable, and being a disease traced to some morbid alteration of structure or function. Mr. C. Spooner considers that "in the majority of cases it is owing to *disease* of the great sciatic nerve, which governs the muscles of the hind extremity; nervous energy is thus imperfectly supplied, and, consequently, the more powerful muscles act the most. It is often connected with disease of the hock, and is sometimes preceded by it."

Mr. Youatt says that " it rarely or never fails to deteriorate, and gradually wear out, the animal; therefore, however stylish a rider may feel on his horse, with stringhalt in both hind legs he must consider that he has an unsound horse."

THICKENING OF THE BACK SINEWS is to be considered as unsoundness, as it is the result of a sprain or strain, causing an inflammation and thickening; the disease may continue for months without any lameness, and with nothing to draw attention to it. Mr. Walsh says, that in thickening of the tendon or its sheath, however well the animal might appear to be, yet " at length, an unusually severe day's work sets up active inflammation, the leg rapidly fills, and there is so much lameness as to cause the horse to be thrown."

Mr. Youatt says : " The continuance of any considerable thickness around the sheaths of the tendons, indicates previous violent sprain. This very thickening will fetter the action of the tendons, and, after much quick work, will occasionally renew the inflammation and lameness; therefore, such a horse cannot be sound."

THOROUGHPIN is to be considered as unsoundness, if of an extensive size and causing lameness. On reference to bog-spavin, the reader will find that all the arguments used there are applicable to this disease.

THRUSH is to be considered as unsoundness, as it is productive of canker, which renders the animal totally unfit for any use. Most horses, while suffering with thrush in its mild form, work and travel well, but, as Mr. Youatt remarks, it is a disease, *i. e.*, "inflammation of the lower surface of the inner or sensible frog, and the secretion or throwing out of pus, almost invariably accompanied by a slight degree of tenderness of the frog itself, involving separation of the horn from the parts beneath, and underrunning, ending in the production of fungus and canker, and, ultimately, a diseased state of the foot, destructive of the present, and dangerous to the future usefulness of the animal."

WIND GALLS are to be considered as unsoundness only when they are very large and numerous, and the animal lame thereby.

WIND SUCKER is to be considered as unsoundness, as, although but a vice at first, it becomes so natural to the animal, that he will continue doing it, generally causing indigestion, colic, and tending to lower his condition.

Mr. Williams, from whom we quote, says, that "a wind sucker gathers air into his mouth and swallows it, blowing himself out, sometimes to a tremendous size; a wind sucker, being subject to colic and indigestion, must be considered as unsound."

GREASE, MANGE, RUPTURES or HERNIA of all kinds, ENLARGEMENT OF SINEWS, ATROPHY of any muscle, diseases of any of the internal viscera, lameness of all kinds and degrees, are to be considered as unsoundness during the time the animal is suffering from any of them.

Those defects comprehended under the term BLEMISHES are enumerated by Mr. Armatage as follows:

"Scars, the effects of broken knees; capped hocks, splints, bog-spavin and thoroughpin, when they are very slight; loss of hair from blisters or from scars; enlargements from blows or cutting; specks or streaks in the cornea (eye); and a few other defects unnecessary to mention."

Under the term VICES we comprehend restiveness, shying, bolting, balking repeatedly, running away, kicking, rearing, biting, kicking in the stable or when shoeing, weaving or moving the head from side to side, quidding, chewing the rope of his halter, and slipping the halter.

ON WARRANTY.

In the purchase of a horse, the buyer usually receives, embodied in his receipt, what is termed a WARRANTY. It should be thus expressed:

"Received of Mr. .... this .... day of .... 187 , the sum of .... Dollars for a .... warranted only .... years old, sound, free from vice, and quiet to ride or drive in all harness." Or, "Warranted free from vice and blemish, except ...." Or, "Warranted in every respect, except ...." Or, "Warranted to have been constantly driven both in single and double harness, to have carried a lady, &c., &c."

Following the word "*except,*" there is every opportunity afforded the (honest) vendor of stating what he may know invalidating the warranty, and thereby saving his reputation, as well as of screening himself from the probability of litigation afterwards.

We shall now quote the opinion of Mr. Youatt as to warranty. He says: "A receipt, including merely the word *warranted*, extends only to soundness, *warranted sound*, and goes no further; the age, freedom from vice, and quietness to ride or drive, should be *especially* named."

This warranty (as given above,) comprises every cause of

ON WARRANTY.

unsoundness that can be detected, or that lurks in the constitution at the time of sale, and to every vicious habit that the animal has hitherto shown. To establish a breach of warranty, and to be enabled to tender a return of the horse, and recover the difference of price, the purchaser must prove that it was unsound, or viciously disposed, at the time of sale. In case of cough, the horse must have been heard to cough immediately after the purchase, or as he was led home, or as soon as he had entered the stable of the purchaser. Coughing, even on the following morning, will not be sufficient; for it is possible that he might have caught cold by the change of stabling. If he is lame, it must be proved to arise from a cause that existed before the animal was in the purchaser's possession. No price will imply a warranty, or be equivalent to one; there must be express warranty. A fraud must be proved in the seller, in order that the buyer may be enabled to return the horse, or mantain an action as to the price. The warranty should be given at the time of sale. A warranty, or a promise to warrant the horse given at any period antecedent to the sale, is invalid; for horse-flesh is a very perishable commodity, and the constitution and usefulness of the animal may undergo a considerable change in the space of a few days. A warranty after the sale is *invalid*, for it is given without any legal consideration. In order to complete the purchase, there must be a transfer of the animal, or a memorandum of agreement, or the payment of the earnest money. The least sum will suffice for earnest (say one dollar). No verbal promise to buy or to sell is binding without one of these. The moment either of these is effected, the legal transfer of property or delivery is made, and whatever may happen to the horse, the seller retains or is entitled to the money. If the purchaser exercises any act of ownership, by using the animal without leave of the vendor, or by having any operation performed or any medicine given to him, he makes him his own.

The warranty of a servant is considered to be binding on the master. The weight of authority decides that the master is bound by the act of the servant. Lord Kenyon, however, had some doubt on the subject.

If the horse should be afterwards discovered to have been unsound at the time of warranty, the buyer may tender a return of it, and, if it be not taken back, may bring an action for the price; but the seller is not bound to rescind the contract, unless he has agreed so to do.

Although there is no legal compulsion to give *immediate* notice to the seller of the discovered unsoundness, it will be better for it to be done. The animal should then be tendered at the house or stable of the vendor. If he refuses to receive him, the animal may be sent to a livery stable and sold; and an action for the difference in price may be brought. The keep, however, can be recovered only for the time that necessarily intervened between the tender and the determination of the action. It is not legally necessary to tender a return of the horse as soon as the unsoundness is discovered. The animal may be kept for a *reasonable* time afterwards, and even PROPER MEDICAL MEANS* used to remove the unsoundness; but courtesy, and, indeed, justice, will require that the notice should be given as soon as possible. Although it is stated, on the authority of Lord Loughborough, that "*no length of time elapsed after the sale will alter the nature of a contract originally false,*" yet it seems to have been once thought it

---

* "Proper medical means," in this passage, as well as in law, is to be construed to mean that a Veterinary Surgeon, graduate of some College, must be called in to prescribe, and not one of the quacks in the city.—(ED.)

ON WARRANTY.

was necessary to the action to give notice of the unsoundness in a reasonable time. The cause of action is certainly complete on breach of the warranty.

It used to be supposed that the buyer had no right to have the horse medically treated, and that he would waive the warranty by doing so. The question, however, would be, has he injured or diminished the value of the horse by the treatment? It will generally be prudent for him to refrain from all medical treatment, because the means adopted, however *skillfully* employed, may have an unfortunate effect, or may be misrepresented by ignorant or interested observers.

The purchaser, possibly, may like the horse, notwithstanding his discovered defect; and he may retain, and bring an action for the depreciation in value on account of the unsoundness. Few, however, will do this, because his retaining the horse will cause a suspicion that the defect was of no great consequence, and will give rise to much cavil about the amount of damages: and, after all, very slight damages will probably be obtained.

"I take it to be clear law," says Lord Eldon, "that if a person purchases a horse that is warranted, and it afterwards turns out that the horse was unsound at the time of warranty, the buyer may, if he pleases, keep the horse, and bring an action on the warranty, in which he will have the right to recover the difference between the value of a sound horse, and one with such defects as existed at the time of warranty; or he may return the horse, and bring an action to recover the full money; but in the latter case, the seller has a right to expect that the horse shall be returned to him in the same state he was when sold, and not by any means diminished in value; for if a person keep a warranted article for any length of time after discovering its defects, and then returns it in a worse state than it would have been if returned immediately after such discovery, I think the party can have no defense to an action for the price of the article on the ground of non-compliance with the warranty, but must be left to his action on the warranty to recover the difference in the value of the article warranted, and its value when sold."—*Curtis* vs. *Hannay*, 3 Esp., 83.

When there is no warranty, an action may be brought on the ground of fraud, but this is very difficult to be maintained, and not often hazarded. It will be necessary to prove that the dealer knew of the defect, and that the purchaser was imposed upon by his false representations, or other fraudulent means. If the defect was evident to every eye, the purchaser has no remedy—he should have taken more care; but if a warranty was given that extends to all unsoundness, palpable or concealed, although a person should ignorantly or carelessly buy a blind horse, warranted sound, he may reject it—the warranty is his guard, and prevents him from so closely examining the horse as he otherwise would have done; but if he buys a blind horse, thinking him to be sound, and without a warranty, he has no remedy. Every one ought to exercise common circumspection and common sense.

A man should have a more perfect knowledge of horses than falls to the lot of most, and a perfect knowledge of the vendor too, who ventures to buy a horse without a warranty.

If a person buys a horse warranted sound, and discovering no defect in him, and relying on the warranty, resells him, and the unsoundness is discovered by the second purchaser, and the horse returned to the first purchaser, or an action commenced against him, he has his claim on the first seller, and may demand of him not only the price of the horse, or the difference in value, but every expense that may have been incurred.

Absolute exchanges of one horse for another, or a sum of money being paid in addition by one of the parties, stand on the same ground as simple sales. If there is a warranty on either side, and that is broken, an action may be maintained; if there be no warranty, deceit must be proved.

The trial of horses on sale often leads to disputes. The law is perfectly clear, but the application of it, as in other matters connected with horse-flesh, is attended with glorious uncertainty. The intended purchaser is only liable for damages done to the horse through his own misconduct. The seller may put what restriction he chooses on the trial, and takes the risks of all accidents in the fair use of the horse within such restrictions.

If a horse from a dealer's stable is galloped far and fast, it is probable that he will soon show distress; and if he is pushed further, inflammation and death may ensue. The dealer rarely gets recompensed for this, nor ought he, as he knows the unfitness of his horse, and may thank himself for permitting such a trial; and if it should occur soon after the sale, he runs the risk of having the horse returned, or of an action for its price.

In this, too, he is not much to be pitied. The mischievous and fraudulent practice of dealers, of giving their horses, by over-feeding, a false appearance of muscular substance, leads to the ruin of many a valuable animal. It would be a useful lesson to have to contest in an action or two, the question, whether a horse overloaded with fat can be otherwise than in a state of disease, and consequently unsound.

It is proper, however, to put a limit to what has been too frequently asserted from the bench, that a horse warranted sound must be taken as fit for immediate use, and capable of being immediately put to any fair work. A hunter honestly warranted sound is certainly warranted to be in immediate condition to follow the hounds.

One of the regulations of the Bazaar, in King Street, London, was exceedingly fair, both with regard to the previous owner and the purchaser, viz.:

"When a horse, having been warranted sound, shall be returned within the prescribed period, on account of unsoundness, a certificate from a veterinary surgeon (not one who gave himself that title, but a graduate of some college), particularly describing the unsoundness, must accompany the horse so returned; when, if it be agreed to by the veterinary surgeon of the establishment, the amount received for the horse shall be immediately paid back; but if the surgeon of the establishment should not confirm the certificate, then, in order to avoid further dispute, one of the veterinary surgeons of the college (Royal Veterinary College) shall be called in, and *his* decision shall be final; and the expense of such umpire shall be borne by the party in error."

In "Hippopathology," we find that on warranty certain remarks and opinions are given, which we shall place before the reader.

"Warranty is meant an indemnity against any unsoundness, or a pledge given, commonly in writing, by the vendor to the purchaser, that the horse is sound and quiet, and possesses such and such qualifications; without such indemnification or pledge, the law says, *Caveat emptor*—let the purchaser take the consequences; the rule at law being that everybody who purchases a horse takes him at his own judgment, and has no remedy against the seller, supposing the horse to turn out, upon a future trial, or on a more considerate inspection after the purchase, to be worth less than the sum given; unless he (the purchaser) can *prove* he was induced to purchase by representations *false* within the knowledge of the seller. To fasten a fraud of this nature upon an experienced dealer in horses is, however, a difficult matter." (See "*Tomlin's Popular Law Dictionary for* 1838.")

Warranties are of different kinds; *express* or *implied*, *general* or *special*. An express warranty speaks for itself. And as for an implied warranty, such a thing is hardly known, or, at least, rarely taken advantage of in *horse dealing;* the price paid, however high, not being legally held to be any guaranty of the soundness of the animal; and anything that might transpire between seller and buyer, *implying* warranty, being worth nothing without proof, which, being procured, would render the transaction, in law, tantamount to an express warranty. A *general* warranty extends to all defects and faults known and unknown to the seller; but a *special* warranty is confined in its operation to the parts or particulars *specially* and *specifically* pointed out. A horse may be warranted of such an age; or, having some defect visible upon his limbs, such as a spavin, or a curb, or a fired leg, of which he does not go lame at the time, that defect may be specified, and the horse warranted not (within any reasonable or prescribed period) to become lame in consequence of it. A general warranty, however, affords no protection against such defects as are plain and obvious to everybody, and consequently to the purchaser, no more than a special warranty does against any which are not included or named in the specification. But if, on the sale of a horse, the seller agrees to deliver it sound and free from blemish at the expiration of a specified period, the warranty is broken by a fault in the horse when delivered, although such defect was obvious at the time of sale; and, as some *splints* cause lameness, and others do not, a splint is not one of those plain defects against which a warranty will not indemnify; and when a seller warrants a horse sound at the time of sale, and the horse afterwards becomes lame from the effects of a splint, visible when the horse was bought, it is certain that the warranty is broken. This rule will apply to *spavin*, or to *curb*, or to *windgall*, or, in fact, to any other defect visible at the time of sale; for all warranties can only undertake for the animal's qualifications at the time of sale; none can extend to any subsequent period unless there be a special clause *to deliver the horse free from blemish*, and that delivery be by mutual agreement delayed. (See *Tomlin's Law Dictionary for* 1838.)

With respect to what (oral) declarations of the seller will amount to a warranty, the primary rule for the interpretation of contracts in general is applicable—it depends upon the intention of the parties. A simple affirmation of the goodness of an article is a warranty, provided it (a warranty) appears to have been intended: whereas the sublimest epithets that seller ever employed to recommend his goods to a credulous buyer, will be regarded as the idle* phraseology of the market, unless an intention to warrant actually appear.

Let us now consider how the rights of the parties are affected by the horse being unsound at the time of warranty. The contract being thus broken on the part of the seller, it is at the buyer's option either to treat it as a

---

* As generally made use of in America, when speaking of their articles—"the best in the world"—"the *finest* animal in America."

nullity, and return the horse, or to retain him notwithstanding, and bring an action on the warranty. In the former case, the price paid is the measure of the damages he will be entitled to recover in an action; in the latter, the difference between that price and his real value. If he offer to rescind the contract and return the horse, he may also recover the expenses of his keep; but in order to do this, a positive tender is said to be necessary. No notice of the unsoundness need be given to the vendor, to entitle the vendee to maintain the action; nor is it necessary to bring the action immediately on discovering the unsoundness. But although such a notice be not essential, yet it is always advisable to give it, as the omitting to do so will furnish at the trial a strong presumption that the horse, at the time of sale, was free from the defect complained of, thus rendering the proof of warranty more difficult. Common justice and honesty require that the commodity should be returned at the earliest period, and before it has been so changed by the lapse of time as to make it impossible to ascertain, by proper tests, what were its original properties.

I cannot conclude this subject without advising those who are satisfied with a moderate degree of goodness in a horse to put up with a few trifling faults, as it often happens that the rider or driver is as much in fault as the horse; and after a little use these trivial faults often disappear.

There is no money better expended when purchasing a horse, than the payment of the fee to a *qualified, respectable* veterinary surgeon, one whose professional knowledge enables him to form, and whose *reputation* induces him to give, a correct and honest opinion as to the soundness of a horse; through saving this trifling sum hundreds of dollars have often been subsequently lost. The certificate of a veterinary surgeon, as to the soundness of a horse, does not prevent such horse from being returned, should he afterwards manifest such symptoms as would prove him to be unsound at the time of sale. Cases may occur in which disease may exist in a latent form, and which professional vigilance may be unable to detect. But to one case of this sort there are hundreds in which the unsoundness would have been detected by the veterinary surgeon, though not by the owner or amateur.

There are two grounds on which a horse can be returned and the value recovered: one, a breach of warranty; the other, the proving a fraud. If a horse is warranted sound, free from vice, steady in harness, and five years old, and he proves either unsound, vicious, unsteady in harness, or more or less than five years, the warranty is broken, and the horse returnable. It is of little use the dealer saying that he *will* warrant the horse, unless he actually *does*, and any professions that he may make amount to nothing; thus, though he were to say, "the horse was the soundest animal ever foaled," or, "the gentlest creature that ever looked through a collar," or, the usual term, "the finest in the world," it amounts to nothing, unless he warrants the one or the other of his assertions. A warranty before a witness is better than a written warranty without a witness.

A warranty does not extend to any limited time unless specified accordingly, as at some of the auction marts. In former days it used to be the law to allow a trial of so many weeks for the eyes, and so many for the wind, &c., but such is not the case at present.

The other ground on which a horse can be returned—that of fraud—is more difficult to prove. If a person sells

ON WARRANTY. 45

another a glandered horse at such a price as the animal would have been worth if sound, it is an act of fraud, and the buyer can recover the amount, as well as the damage, should the infection have been communicated to other horses belonging to him; provided, it can be proved that the seller knew that the horse was glandered at the time of sale (no matter if he was not warranted), it is absolutely a case of fraud. If any gross deception be practiced to hide a fault, the horse is returnable on the ground of fraud, though no warranty be given. It is necessary, however, that the fault afterward discovered should not be of such glaring description that any man of common judgment would have readily discovered, such as a large blemish on the knee, or the absence of an eye; for the law expects the purchaser to exercise common vigilance. In cases where there exists some temporary unsoundness, it is desirable to have such defect mentioned in the warranty—the horse to be returnable, or a fair allowance made, if the unsoundness becomes permanent.

In cases where there is an unsoundness, but one to which the purchaser does not object, it is desirable that a qualified warranty should be given—that is, sound in every other respect but this *one* exception.

In obtaining a warranty, let it be written and signed by the seller *himself* if possible; for, if you should have reason to commence a suit to recover damages from the horse proving unsound, he might swear that he did not read it when he signed it, nor did he instruct his clerk to give the warranty as it is written, &c.; not that such a statement of the seller is worth much, but as these cases are generally decided by the jury system, which does not generally decide cases by the weight of evidence, this plan will be found very useful should any defect afterward appear which may render it necessary to return the horse. It is thought necessary by many persons, when a horse is returned, to put him into the stable of the seller, or to get him to receive the horse; but it has been established in our courts of law that this is not necessary, and that it is sufficient to give notice by a witness that the horse is unsound or vicious, or is not what he was warranted to be, and that he is ready to be delivered up when sent for; although, by tendering the horse, and afterwards placing him at livery, the keep of an unsound horse after this tender can be recovered; this is, therefore, the best plan to adopt when the seller is a solvent and responsible man. If the horse is sold to a third party, an action can be brought, after due notice given to the vendor, for the difference between the price given and the price the horse sold for, after deducting all expenses that were actually necessary in the keep of the animal, and at the sale; the best and most advisable plan is to sell the horse at a mart, or otherwise, by auction, due notice having been given to the seller.

It is advisable, after purchasing, not to have the horse shod, nor to give him any medicine, until satisfied, by a sufficient trial, that he is in every respect sound.

Perhaps I have dwelt longer upon this subject than some of my readers may think necessary; but it should be recollected that it is intended only for those who are inexperienced in horses. It may be thought, also, that what I have written may tend to excite an unjust prejudice in the minds of those to whom it is addressed, or that it may make them over-cautious, and induce them to reject horses without sufficient reason; but if we take into consideration the many defects or diseases to which horses are liable, the difficulty of detecting them, the numerous deceptions that are practiced, and the shifts and evasions sometimes resorted to, I trust that, in what I have written, the candid reader will not accuse me of having gone too far, or that it will excite an undue prejudice against the horse-dealer. I am aware that there are men in that trade who would descend to the deceptive practices that I treat on in another part of this book, but have no doubt that there are also to be found among them, men of strict integrity and honor.

ADVICE TO BUYERS.

In this division of the subject we propose to treat of the precautions to be observed in purchasing horses, and to explain the various devices practiced by unprincipled dealers to deceive the inexperienced and unwary. The information and advice here introduced is mainly gathered from the experiences of Messrs. Armatage, Mason, Spooner, Gamgee, Youatt, and Blain—who are high authority on all matters pertaining to horse-flesh—together with the results of our own observations and practice.

It is a very ancient but valuable maxim, that in all transactions, "*honesty is the best policy*," and I can see no reason whatever why horse-dealing should not be regulated by this excellent law.

I have known some persons who have persisted in the practice of never giving a warranty with a horse, and have experienced the advantage of it; for it is evident that few who have had any use for a horse would sell it unless it had some fault; and if we go to a horse-dealer to purchase a horse of five or six years of age, it is but reasonable to conclude that the horse may have been tried by some other person, and sold for some fault; still, it should be recollected that there are few, if any horses, without some fault or imperfection; and perhaps, if the qualifications of riders or drivers (even the best) were strictly inquired into, they would be found equally deficient; we had better, therefore, go upon the principle of getting a horse that has no SERIOUS fault or defect, or what may be fairly deemed unsoundness; and having purchased such a horse, we should ride or drive him a few days or weeks, and not be too hasty in giving an opinion of him, nor too ready in listening to the opinions or criticisms of others, as there will always be found many ready to give their voluntary opinion, no matter how ignorant they may be as regards their judgment of a horse; and, as I remarked before in another chapter, the more ignorant the person is, the more capable he thinks himself; I have always found this fact established, more particularly as to horses. Having premised thus much, I will proceed to give some further advice, or suggest some precautions, which may be profitably recollected by the purchaser of horses.

The numerous shades which exist between a state of perfect soundness in horses, and those obvious diseases or defects which so clearly constitute unsoundness as to admit of no doubt on the subject, often occasion much trouble and perplexity in the purchase or sale of these animals.

If a person, inexperienced in the mysteries of horse-dealing, wishes to purchase a horse, he would do well to consult a *professional* man (not the quacks that generally overrun every city), or, in preference to the latter, some friend, even if he does not know very much of the horse, but of whose honesty you are satisfied; but, at any rate, consult some honest person, capable of guarding you against any deception that might be attempted, and of

ADVICE TO BUYERS.

pointing out any defects that may be of too obscure a nature to attract your notice. When such assistance cannot be procured, the following hints will be found undoubtedly useful.

It would be useless to attempt a minute examination of a horse while the dealer or his assistant are present; the sloping ground upon which the horse stands for examination gives a deceptive view of his form and height, while the constant fear he feels of the whip, and the high-flown panegyrics lavished upon him, are so perplexing to a person unaccustomed to the business, that he is apt to overlook the most palpable defects; nor is it possible for the most experienced to examine him with all the accuracy and attention that are necessary, as an unobserved flourish of the whip, or some other private hint from the seller, or some of his assistants, may keep the horse constantly in motion, particularly when the eye happens to be directed to a part that he does not wish to be inspected. I do not mean to say that this is always the case; there are many dealers, no doubt, of strict integrity, who afford ample opportunity to those who wish to examine their horses, and so far from wishing to practice any deception upon the inexperienced, will never warrant a horse sound unless they are convinced that he is really so; but that there are men in the business who have recourse to a variety of tricks to deceive the unwary, is too notorious to be doubted. It is advisable, therefore, after taking a general view of the animal, so as to be satisfied with respect to his figure and action, to ride him off to some convenient place, where he may be examined without interruption.

In a book published a few years ago on this subject, by Mr. R. Lawrence, he observes that "there are two kinds of horse-dealers—the common, and the gentleman dealer;

and that there is this distinction between them: the former is obliged to warrant a horse sound *before* he can sell him, whereas the latter simply says that he believes the horse to be sound, and that it is not customary with him to give a warranty. Thus, the first is bound by *law ;* the latter by *honor ;* nevertheless there are some *eccentric and narrow-minded purchasers,* who, in spite of the numerous bright examples of modern honor, prefer the former mode of dealing to the latter.

The first and most important point to be inquired into, is the state of the feet and limbs, and whether the horse be in any degree lame or not. And though it appear perfectly firm, and free from lameness in all its paces, it will be necessary to inspect carefully the feet and limbs, lest there be any defect, which, at some future time, may occasion lameness. It is a fact, pretty well known to horse-dealers, that a slight degree of lameness is easily concealed, particularly in high-spirited horses, by the use of a stimulus, (whip or spur, etc.), and supporting the head with the bridle, so as to keep it high. To ascertain, therefore, whether a horse be lame or not, he should not be ridden, but a person should be made to run before him, holding the end of the bridle, so that the head may receive no support from it; the slightest lameness will then be readily perceived, particularly if the trial be made on rough ground, and on a moderate declivity.

Should it appear that the horse is perfectly free from lameness, the feet and legs are to be carefully inspected, beginning with the former, which should be first viewed in front, as the horse stands, to observe if there be any difference in the form or size of the hoofs. If the feet are very small, and particularly if one foot appears smaller than the other, it affords reasonable cause for suspicion that there is

ADVICE TO BUYERS.

some defect; the bottom of the foot is then to be examined, and if the heels are much *contracted*, the *frog imperfect*, and matter issuing from its cleft or division, it is probable that the horse will soon become lame. I would not advise that a horse be rejected merely because the feet have become rather narrow at the heels, or a little smaller than they were originally, unless RINGS or grooves are found around the foot near to the coronet; in such a case, you might suspect that the horse has been attacked with inflammation of the foot, and the disease might return on one or two days' hard work.

If no difference can be perceived in the size of the feet, if the frogs appear sound and free from thrushes, and particularly if, at the same time, the horse step boldly and firmly when trotted on *rough* ground, and down a hill, I think he may be safely purchased, if free from all other defects.

The next point to be attended to is the form of the sole or bottom of the foot, which is, in its natural state, rather hollow or concave: we sometimes, however, find it quite flat, or even convex; in either case it is proportionally thin, and unfit for the office it seems to be designed for, that is, to protect the sensible or fleshy sole which it covers. The flat sole, however, is by no means so serious a defect as the convex, and, if the horse is carefully shod, seldom occasions lameness; but when the sole is in any degree convex, or projecting, it is extremely thin, and incapable of bearing much pressure. A horse with this defect will sometimes step firmly, when the sole is protected by a wide, hollow shoe; but he is continually liable to become lame by gravel under the sole. We generally find, on this kind of foot, that the front of the hoof, or wall, has lost its natural form, having become flatter; it is thinner and more brittle than it is naturally, so that it is difficult to nail a shoe on securely without wounding or pricking the foot, as it is termed. This defect, therefore, is of a serious nature, and constitutes a class of unsoundness. In examining the fore-feet, we should attentively observe whether there are any corns. We can sometimes discover this without taking off the shoes, but by no means so well as when they are removed. If the corns are *slight*, they do not form a sufficient objection to an otherwise good horse; but if they are extensive, and particularly if the heels are likewise weak, the horse should be rejected.

Sand-crack is an important defect, when it runs longitudinally from the coronet into the hoof, and is so deep as to affect the sensible parts of the foot; sometimes, however, it is very superficial, or in a horizontal direction, and perhaps too trifling to deserve notice. It should be recollected, however, that these trifling cracks in the hoof indicate an unnatural dryness of the horn, and, consequently a tendency to sand-crack; therefore, when such a horse is purchased, proper means should be employed to improve the state of the hoof.

There is no part of the horse which requires a more careful inspection than the foot; for it sometimes happens that lameness is for a time removed by rest, or a run at grass, and may not again appear until the horse is put to work. Horses that are foundered, are generally much relieved, and sometimes apparently cured, by running at grass; but the lameness invariably returns when the horse is worked, or kept in a stable floored with planks, or bricked.

A horse's foot may have suffered so far by bad shoeing, improper management, or some unknown cause, that although lameness may not have taken place at the time of purchase, yet, from the appearance of the foot, it may

ADVICE TO BUYERS. 53

reasonably be suspected that he will soon become lame. Should such a horse be purchased with a warranty of soundness, he could not perhaps be legally returned, if lameness take place two or three weeks afterwards, as the seller would be able to prove that the horse had not been lame up to the time he was purchased. It may be said, perhaps, that the defect in the foot was observed at that time, but it is well known that we rarely meet with a horse, at the age of seven or eight, whose feet are not more or less imperfect, caused principally from bad shoeing, and that a considerable alteration in form sometimes takes place without causing lameness. Another point, special attention should be called to. After purchasing your horse with a good and sound foot, try and avoid all *fancy* shoers, who think that cutting out the sole, paring away the frog, placing on nice-looking small shoes, and finally using the rasp to finish their disgraceful jobs, is perfection. Let the sole alone, except when absolutely required. Do not touch the frog, and do not allow the rasp to be too freely used. All that is required is simply to take off the roughness of the old shoeing, and for the purpose of clinching the nails, and to go no higher than the clinch.

Cutting is a defect often met with; and when it is considerable—that is, when the scar on the inside of the fetlock is large, the parts surrounding thickened, and if it appears also to have been recently wounded—it must be deemed a serious imperfection. Cutting on the inside and immediately below the knee joint (speedy cut, as it is termed), is also a material defect, as it sometimes causes a horse to fall suddenly, or he may become so lame as to be almost useless.

The back sinews are next to be examined, by passing the hand down the back part of the leg. If the tendon or sinew can be distinctly felt, with the suspensory ligament which lies immediately before it, if the tendon feel clean and free from swelling, and if the leg, on a side view, appear flat, clean and sinewy, as it is termed, it may be considered as a sound, well-formed leg. But if the leg, on a side view, appears rather round than flat, or rather bent and inclined inwards, if the sinew and ligament cannot be distinctly felt, and particularly if one leg is larger than the other, it may be concluded that the part has sustained some injury, and that there is a probability of the horse becoming lame when put to any hard work. If any mark be found on the knees, it is the safest plan to infer that it was occasioned by falling, through some weakness of the joint, though the seller should affirm that it happened in going over a bar, stepping on or off the boat, or by striking it against the manger.

Few horses are entirely free from splints—they need not, therefore, be regarded, unless of a large size immediately below the knee, or so near the back sinew or suspensory ligament as to interfere with their action, or unless they are tender on being pressed.

In examining the hind-legs, begin with the hock, and if there be any spavin it may be seen most readily by looking between the hocks, or, still better, by looking between the fore-legs, rather inclining to one side. The bones, which form the projection on the inside of the hock, are in some horses rather larger than in others; this should not be mistaken for bone-spavin, but there is no great difficulty in making the distinction, for, should both hocks be affected with spavin, it rarely happens that they are exactly alike, or of the same size; and when one hock only is affected, the difference is sufficiently manifest to point out the disease. A side view of the hocks should next be taken, and if there be a curb it will be readily perceived.

Observe, in the next place, if there be any ringbone on the pastern, which, though a considerable defect, does not always produce lameness, but more frequently in the fore-leg than the hind.

In examining the bottom of the hind-foot, we have to ascertain that it is not affected with canker, bad thrushes, and the other defects treated on in regard to the fore-feet.

Some horses have a tendency to swelling of the hind-legs, or to that discharge from the heels which constitutes the disease termed "scratches;" and horses with white legs seem to be more disposed to this complaint than others. When a horse's hind-legs, therefore, appear to be swollen, if the hair about the heels appear rough or furzy, or if there be scars on the heels, or an appearance of their having been affected with cracks or ulcers, it may be inferred that the horse is subject to scratches and swelling of the legs; do not omit to observe if there be any puffs on the inner part of the hock, a little to the front; if so, and they are tender to the touch, and evince pain to the animal, or any heat can be felt in them, it would be better not to run the risk of taking an animal that might be very lame on one or two days' hard work, and when these puffs (also known as bog-spavin) cause lameness, although it is in but few cases that they do so, they generally are very troublesome and difficult to treat.

Having finished our examination of the feet and limbs, we should proceed to the eye, which is an important part, and requires the most careful inspection. The most favorable situation for viewing the eye is at the stable door, or under a shed; for when too much light falls upon the eye, so much is reflected by its cornea, or surface, that it is difficult to see the external part. I am not treating of a blind horse, for any person must be blind themselves not to detect a blind horse, but it is on signs and indications, that will cause you to suspect that the animal will go blind after being a little while in your possession.

The age at which the eyes most frequently become diseased is from five to six; next to that, from four to five; sometimes, but not often, it happens after six; after seven the disease rarely occurs, except from accidents, to which, of course, they are equally exposed at all ages. In purchasing a horse, therefore, about five years old, it is necessary to be particularly attentive to the state of the eyes. If they appear dull, cloudy, or watery, if the lids appear to be more closed than usual, if the inner corner of the eyelid appears puckered up, and particularly if there is a manifest difference in the appearance of the eyes, they may justly be suspected to be unsound.

Having taken a general view of the eye, the pupil, or dark bluish oblong spot in its centre, should be closely and carefully examined; and if a difference is perceived in the size of the two pupils—if, instead of a dark blue color, they appear cloudy, or if white specks are seen in them—a diseased state of the organs is indicated. Mr. Armatage says, "I have observed in many instances, that when a small speck has formed in the pupil, it does not gradually increase, as by many it is supposed to do; on the contrary, I have, in many cases, known it remain in the same state for years without causing any material impediment to vision." I should not, therefore, reject a horse simply on account of this defect; that is, if the eyes appeared perfectly healthy in every other respect, and particularly if the speck is small, nearer the edge than the centre of the pupil, and only in one eye; it would be advisable, however, that the fact be understood that the pupils become small when the eyes are exposed to a strong light, and enlarge again when the horse is brought into a darker situation; so that if the light is allowed to fall more strongly on one eye than on the other, the former will appear smaller.

When an imperfection is observed in the eye, it is frequently said to arise from a bite, or blow, or from hay seeds falling into it; but, though the seller should positively affirm this to be the cause of the imperfection, I should always be inclined to doubt it, because experience has taught me that the diseases of the horse's eye almost always arise from internal causes; that, however trifling in appearance, they are really of a serious nature, and most commonly, even after they have been apparently cured, terminate, sooner or later, in blindness. Too much caution, therefore, cannot be observed in examining this important part. There is a disease, to which the eye is subject, termed "gutta serena," or glass eye, which, although the horse be totally blind in either one or both eyes, it is difficult to be noticed by an inexperienced person, as there are no specks nor any dullness about the eye; in fact, just the contrary; but, on close examination, if one eye be affected, you will find the lids somewhat more apart than the other eye, and there will be more of a sort of staring appearance about it, and the eye itself will have a more glossy aspect than natural; but if both eyes are diseased, you will find greater difficulty in detecting it, as both eyes will then be alike in size and appearance; but you must in this case take notice of the size of the pupil while in the dark, and bring the horse towards the light, and if you see no difference in the size of the pupil, the horse is blind, as the pupil should become smaller when exposed to the light, and, besides, the horse will raise his feet a little higher than ordinary.

When the eyes become inflamed from a blow or bite, or from any dust getting into them, the disease, although apparently considerable, is seldom of long continuance; that is, when the injury is not severe and proper means are employed for its removal. But when the inflammation has subsided, there often remains on the surface of the eye an opaque spot, or film, which in severe injuries extends over the whole of the cornea or surface of the eye. After a little time, this opacity gradually diminishes, and sometimes wholly disappears; more commonly, however, a small film remains, which does not in any material degree impede vision. This defect, therefore, is of no importance, and may safely be overlooked, provided the purchaser is certain that the opacity is really on the surface, and not in the pupil of the eye, and that the other parts appear bright, and free from every kind of imperfection. As a further security, a condition may be annexed to the warranty, by which the horse may be returned in three or four months, should the imperfection prove to be of a serious nature. When a complete cataract takes place, which is known by the pupil being of a white or pearl color, the strength of the other eye is generally restored, and it rarely becomes diseased afterwards, except from accidents; he may, therefore, be safely purchased as a *one-eyed horse.*

We have now to extend our investigation to another point: that is, the state of the wind, or rather of the lungs, and of the parts connected with them.

When a horse is absolutely broken-winded, there is no difficulty in detecting the disease; the laborious breathing, or working of the flanks, particularly in going up a hill, and the short, asthmatic cough, are symptoms which cannot escape observation. Between this state of the lungs and perfect health there are many degrees, and it is the intermediate defects that we find most difficulty in discovering.

The criterion by which dealers judge of the state of a horse's wind is by no means a bad one—they make the horse cough by pinching or grasping the top of the windpipe; if the lungs are in that state which constitutes broken-wind, or if they are approaching to that state, the sound of the cough is so peculiar that it cannot well be mistaken—it is short and husky, exactly like that of an asthmatic person. When this kind of cough is observed, the horse should be rejected, even if the motion of the flanks appear perfectly easy and regular. " I have known," says Mr. Spooner, "in several instances, broken-wind apparently cured, by keeping a horse at grass; that is, he seemed to breathe with ease, and did not cough when moderately exercised, but by pinching the throat there was that peculiar cough, and by keeping him in the stable a few days he became as bad as ever."

It is advisable, therefore, for those who have occasion to purchase horses, to make themselves familiar with the sound of this asthmatic or broken-winded cough; there will be no difficulty in this, as the complaint is very common, and horses are more liable to coughs than other domestic animals. The complaint is sometimes of little importance, and with care, easily removed; it often proves, however, extremely obstinate, and not unfrequently incurable.

When a horse is observed to have a cough at the time of purchase, it is necessary to inquire whether it be a recent complaint, or one of long standing ; and this is a point that cannot be always easily determined.

In the old, or chronic cough, as it is termed, the horse generally appears lively, feeds heartily, and appears in every other respect to be in perfect health. Sometimes the sound of the cough is husky, or asthmatic, which indicates a tendency to broken-wind; more commonly it is loud and clear; the fit of coughing is generally violent, and the horse often appears as if some extraneous body had got into the wind-pipe, and he was endeavoring to cough it up.

The chronic cough is most considerable when the horse is first put in motion; by continuing the exercise it gradually ceases, after which the horse may be ridden a long journey without coughing. I have often observed that horses with chronic cough are very shy of having their throats touched, often rearing and making considerable resistance when any one attempts to make them cough by grasping the top of the wind-pipe; and "in many instances," says Mr. Armatage, "I have observed that they cannot be made to cough, in cases of a chronic nature, by squeezing the top of the wind-pipe, however strong the grasp may be." This, probably, as well as the shyness they manifest on the occasion, may arise from the trial having been often made upon them.

In the recent cough the horse generally appears rather dull and heavy, and looks like a horse laboring under a catarrh or cold; he readily coughs when the wind-pipe is pinched, in doing which there is no difficulty, as the horse seldom makes any considerable resistance.

When the cough is of recent date, the horse is sometimes relieved by throwing up mucous through the nostrils, and the cough is often so much moderated by strict attention to his diet and exercise, as to appear scarcely worth notice. When a horse, therefore, is observed to have a cough, the purchaser may not always be able to determine whether the complaint be unimportant, or of long standing and incurable. In such doubtful cases, it would perhaps be the most prudent plan to reject the animal, unless you can secure a suitable condition to the warranty.

There is another complaint of the lungs, or parts connected with them, and an incurable one, which the purchaser should be guarded against—this disease is named *roaring*, from the wheezing noise a horse that is thus affected makes when ridden fast, particularly when galloped up a hill; it is sometimes so considerable as to be heard at a distance of many yards, but in walking, or moderate exercise, it can seldom be perceived. The method which is usually adopted to detect this complaint, when sufficient time is not allowed to have the horse properly examined, is to whip him under the belly, and make him turn suddenly, or by making him leap over a bar; if he is a roarer, this sudden exertion causes him to grunt sufficiently loud and plainly to be easily detected. But this criterion should never be depended upon when an opportunity offers of either galloping the horse, or having him properly tested in the other various ways.

Another defect to which attention must be called, is regarding injuries. After you have examined the animal in the manner already laid down, place the animal on very even ground, especially the hind-legs, then stand immediately behind the animal, to view the hind-parts; see if both sides of the rump are even, that the point of one hip is not lower than the other, that the muscles on one side are not flatter than on the other side; if all appear perfect, then try if the animal has use of his tail, as it is a common occurrence to see fine-looking animals lose, from an injury, the use of their tails, and from the want of it in the summer months, dwindle away to a mere skeleton. The manner to detect it is by pricking him under the belly, and if he has use of it, he will swing it, or you may feel it, and easily detect if he has any use of it. Before you complete your examination, take a step to the side of the animal, and place your hand over the loins, and press steadily; do not insert your finger-nails into the horse's flesh, and exclaim, "He flinches!" but press steadily, and if a *horse*, and he gives or crouches, it is suspicious that he either is affected in his kidneys, or that he has received some injury that may at a future time render him unfit for work; if it be a *mare*, then, before you reject her, her crouching must be considerable, and she must evince some degree of pain, as most mares will crouch a little on pressure on their kidneys, especially during their season.

As to age, I shall treat of it in another place, but it is always advisable to have the age of the horse expressed on the warranty, as you can then avail yourself of the first opportunity that offers of obtaining correct information on the subject, and, if you have been deceived, you will have the right to return the animal.

Mr. Spooner says "that he has known persons so cautious, when about to purchase a horse, as to examine the neck, and if they find marks of his having been bled often, they suspect, sometimes justly, that he has had some serious complaint. They have also thought it necessary to inspect the chest, belly, and thighs, or the parts where rowels or setons are usually placed, and if they observe the marks which generally remain after roweling, they suspect it was done for a complaint of the eyes, when the mark is under the throat, or between the branches of the under jaw-bone; and if in other parts, for what they term *humors*, that is, swelling of the legs, or grease."

Having fininshed our examination of the horse as it relates to soundness, we have next to inquire if he has any

ADVICE TO BUYERS. 63

vicious habits, such as crib-biting, wind-sucking, kicking when shoeing, chewing the rope of his halter, or slipping his halter, and be guarded against them, by the warranty; but if the horse appear to suit in every respect, I would not advise rejecting him on account of some trivial vice that may be rectified by care, such as kicking when shoeing, chewing the rope, or slipping his halter; but a crib-biter and wind-sucker I would never recommend any one to purchase, except at a very reduced figure, and we must further inquire if he is in any degree restive. Crib-biting and wind-sucking are vicious habits, which often cause a horse to become lean and weak, and sometimes render him very subject to flatulent colic. It is, therefore, a defect of importance. In crib-biting he lays hold of the manger, post, or stump of a tree with his teeth, and appears to be sucking with an almost convulsive effort, and a slight grunting noise. The manner in which this injures a horse has not been satisfactorily explained, but it is allowed by all to be an important defect. Wind-sucking can be easily understood by the name; the horse will suck in air while standing in the centre of his box-stall; he gives a sort of convulsive twitch with his lips, and you will observe him to swallow the air, and extend his head a little to one side; he also can suck in air by laying hold of the manger, &c.; but it is not all crib-biters that are also wind-suckers. It may be easily detected by watching the horse for a short time in his stall undisturbed.

Restiveness is sometimes discovered by separating a horse from his companion after riding together a few miles, or after riding him and bringing him back to his stable, by attempting to ride him off again; on these occasions, if a horse has any restiveness, he generally exhibits it.

Before I close this subject, it may be proper to remind

the reader that we rarely meet with a horse that is in every respect perfect; and though, from the high price of the animal, it is necessary to be very cautious, yet it is possible, perhaps, to carry our caution too far; that is, there may be some trifling imperfection, such as a small splint, which is not worth noticing. One caution I always think necessary, however perfect the horse may appear, and that is, to have the receipt and warranty in the handwriting of the seller, stating that the horse is warranted sound, and free from vice, &c, &c.

The next caution, or exposure of the various devices practiced by the tricky horse-dealer, I shall now place before the reader.

When a dealer finds that his horse has a bad cough, and he expects some *greenhorn*, as they call those persons who are inexperienced in the art of horse-trading, to be there the next day to try the horse, he will administer two drachms of powdered opium the night before; and, on the morning of the day that the purchaser is expected, three and sometimes four drachms are given. This medicine acts to check the irritation for a day or so, therefore the cough is perfectly absent on the day that he is purchased; and if, after a day or two, the purchaser finds that he has a horse with a very severe cough, he will go to the seller and make the statement; but unless the purchaser can prove that medicine was given the horse in order to deceive him, he has no redress.

In many instances a dealer will have a horse with a discharge from his nostrils, but knows well enough that to offer such a horse would be the means of exciting a suspicion that the animal might be getting glanders, or some other serious disease; he will, therefore, administer four drachms sulphate of iron three times a day, and keep the nostrils clear, and after four to eight days he will have the animal ready for sale, as the discharge will be dried up, and the animal somewhat improved under the use of this tonic; but how long will the animal's nostrils remain clean? Just as soon as the horse is exposed to the slightest degree of cold it will return with greater severity; and if it was the forerunner of some serious disease, will in a measure be the means of keeping it off for a little while, but, eventually, the animal will fall a martyr to the disease.

Another plan for deceiving the inexperienced is adopted when a dealer happens to have for sale a horse a little tender, or lame, in one leg; he will slightly affect the other leg, so that the horse will travel evenly, and not show any lameness on the diseased foot; the manner in which this is done is by taking off the shoe from the sound leg, and paring a spot on the sole of the foot on which the shoe will rest, then replace the shoe, so as to press on the tender spot and give the animal a slight pain, sufficient to cause the pain of both feet to be equal; then the animal will not be lame at all, but he will travel a little short with both feet, and the purchaser will be told that such is the natural action of the horse; but in a great many instances the horse travels so well that it is not at all noticed, unless you have seen the animal walk before he was fixed in that manner.

Many horses, after an attack of rheumatism of the chest, founder, &c., are troubled with an ugly hollow chest, sinking away in; such a horse is generally very difficult to sell at a figure to compensate a dealer; but he resorts to a plan to give the horse a fine full chest, which will deceive the inexperienced, but is easily detected by a careful examination; he will puncture the chest, and with care separate the skin from the flesh, then he will insert a hollow tube, and blow out the chest as large as he desires; he will then withdraw the tube, stitch up the orifice, place a plaster over it, and after a few days the place will heal up, leaving the chest quite full and prominent, which will remain so until the animal is put to work. They have also resorted to this plan to equalize the appearance of hocks, or to fill up a lop-sided horse where the muscles of one side have wasted away.

They have a plan of giving white or cream-colored horses black marks, so that they match well in appearance, such as, all black legs, a black star, black mane or tail, or certain attractive black spots on the body; the method of doing this is to take six ounces of litharge, quicklime twelve ounces, powder them very finely, then mix them together, place it into a pan, and pour on it sharp lye, then boil it, and you will find a fatty substance floating on the top, which skim off, and use to rub the horse in such places as you desire to have black, and it will become black almost immediately.

It will also change hair that is bay, or chestnut, or sorrel, to a black, with only this difference, viz.: Take six ounces of litharge, and quicklime six ounces, and use fresh water instead of the lye—to be used as the other. The coloring of such colored horses may require a second application, but, in most instances, the parts will be black by the next morning.

Many dealers have a pair of horses that match well in every respect, except that one has a large star on his forehead, and the other has none; he will, to give both a star, take a razor and shave off the hair from the horse without the star, to the size and shape he wishes; then he will take a small quantity of oil of vitriol, and with a brush paint the part once, which will be quite sufficient; after the part becomes sore he will heal it up with copperas water, and after it has healed up both horses will be starred alike.

There are some dealers who even go a little further than ordinary means to deceive the unwary; for instance, if some gay fellow comes along, and wants a fine, dashing, stylish horse, *that can go*, the dealer will take a little turpentine and rub inside the thighs, and when the gay fellow takes up his lines to try him, he will say on his return that he never drove a more dashing animal, and will make the purchase only to find out that the next day he has a dull, heavy brute of an animal.

Before I close this chapter, I have one more remark to make, and as our next division treats on the age of horses, shall only here expose another of the devices practiced to deceive the inexperienced. The age of a horse is known by certain marks in the teeth.

When these are worn out by age, artificial marks are sometimes made, to make the horse appear younger than he really is. It often happens, also, that some of the sucking, or colt's teeth, are drawn out, in which case they are soon replaced by horse's, or permanent teeth; this is done with a view to make a horse of three or four years old appear to be five.

ON AGE AND APPEARANCE.

The horse has, at five years old, forty teeth, viz., twenty-four molar or jaw teeth (twelve in each jaw, and six on each side), twelve incisors, or front teeth, being six in each jaw, and four tushes, one on either side of each jaw, and situated between the molar and incisor teeth. In mares the tushes are generally absent, and sometimes there are a few supplementary teeth.

The teeth are placed in very deep sockets in the jaw-bones, by which, with the assistance of the gums, they are firmly kept in their situation.

The structure of the teeth is very curious. In the horse we find it composed of three portions—first, the bone, or rather the ivory, for it is similar to the tusks of the elephant, forms the bulk of the tooth; secondly, the enamel, which is exceedingly hard, and forms the surface of the crown and a portion of the face, and dips into the body of the tooth; thirdly, the crusta petrosa, softer than the other portions, and more opaque. This portion appears to be a sort of cement to unite the other constituents together, but it is only found in herbivorous animals.

In the fœtus of three or four months old, we find the germ of the first pair of teeth in the alveolar cavity; it appears a soft pulpy substance secreted by a membranous capsule, which in an incisor tooth is single, but in the molar there are no less than four to the under, and five to the upper, which accounts for the irregular appearance of the molar teeth. The pulp is gradually changed into the hard material. The membrane of the incisor teeth that secreted the pulp is double, and from its outer surface it afterwards secretes the enamel, and from its inner the ivory. A tooth is divided into crown and fang, the former being that portion outside the gum, and the latter that contained within the socket; whilst the part immediately embraced by the gum is called the neck. The upper surface of the crown is called the face, and is that part on which the *mark* is situated in the incisor, by which we judge of the age.

Before the age of five, the age of the horse is ascertained

by the presence or disappearance of the temporary teeth; and from five to eight by the disappearance of the mark, which is commonly supposed to be filled up, but in fact disappears by the borders of the cavity being worn down. It takes about three years to wear the teeth down to the bottom of these cavities; thus, the anterior or front teeth, being first formed, are first to lose their mark; the middle teeth following the next, and the corner teeth the succeeding year. The French distinguish the incisor teeth by calling the anterior ones the *nippers*, the corner teeth the *corners*, and those between them the *dividers;* which terms will serve to distinguish them in this place. When the incisors first appear, the anterior border of the cavity is somewhat higher than the posterior internal border; but in the course of a year it is worn down level.

For many years it has been customary to judge the age of the horse by marks in the teeth, but at eight years old the horse loses those marks, and is said to be aged; and after this time it was considered to be *impossible* to ascertain the age. There are, however, other means which will enable us pretty generally to judge of the age, if not with certainty, at any rate approaching to it. If we take an incisor tooth and make three or four transverse sections of it, we shall find that each surface is of a different shape. The tooth becomes gradually less from side to side and more from front to rear; at a certain depth it becomes triangular, and, lower still, the oval appears almost reversed, the diameter being less from side to side than from front to rear. Each of these several portions of the tooth becomes, in the course of time, its face, the shape of which therefore enables us to approximate to the age. This is still more assisted, up to a certain age, by the fact that the enamel that forms the side of the infundibulum dips deeper into the tooth than the cavity within it. It may therefore be seen in the centre of the face for some years after the disappearance of the mark.

Mr. Armatage says: "The funnels in the upper incisor teeth being deeper, and the wear being less than in the under teeth, the marks are longer disappearing. It has been stated that there are two years' space between the disappearance of the marks in the different teeth; the middle teeth losing at ten, the dividers at twelve, and the corners at fourteen; but this is a matter of much irregularity and uncertainty. Their presence and disappearance will, however, serve to assist the other signs in informing us of the age."

The following are the changes by which we judge of the age of a horse. It is unnecessary to notice the molar teeth, as they cannot be readily examined, nor the upper incisors, as their changes are very uncertain:

AT BIRTH, the nippers only have made their appearance.

AT ONE YEAR OLD, the nippers and dividers are very plain and visible; the corners are also visible, having last appeared.

AT TWO YEARS OLD, the nippers have lost their marks, and both edges of the corners are level.

AT THREE YEARS OLD, and several months before, the permanent nippers have made their appearance.

AT FOUR YEARS OLD, the permanent dividers appear, and the cavity has nearly disappeared in the temporary corners.

AT FIVE YEARS OLD, the mouth is said to be perfect, and, if a male, the tushes are up; the permanent corner teeth have appeared, but the posterior border of the cavity is much lower than the anterior, and the mark is much diminished in the nippers.

AT SIX YEARS OLD, the mark has disappeared from the nippers, and considerably diminished in the dividers, but the inner edge of the corners is not yet level.

AT SEVEN YEARS OLD, the mark has disappeared from the nippers and dividers, and the corners are level, though still retaining the mark.

AT EIGHT YEARS OLD, the mark has disappeared from the corners also, and the horse is said to be aged. The face of the teeth is becoming more oval, but the enamel, the remains of the funnel, is still to be seen in the centre of the face.

AT NINE YEARS OLD, the nippers become rounder and the dividers oval; the following year the dividers become round, and the next year the corners assume their shape; the central enamel gradually diminishes.

AT TWELVE YEARS OLD, the central enamel has disappeared; sometimes, however, it remains for some years. The marks in the upper teeth by this time have disappeared, some say at eleven years old, but this is uncertain.

AT FIFTEEN YEARS OLD, the nippers have become triangular, having been gradually assuming this shape for the last two years. The following year the dividers also assume this shape.

AT SEVENTEEN YEARS OLD, the lower incisors are all triangular, and the central enamel has disappeared from the upper incisor. After this the face of the teeth lengthen from front to rear, and diminish from side to side.

There is another method of ascertaining the age of a horse, and we have found it to be invariably correct; but it requires some practice, so as to be able to distinguish the wrinkles, as in full and prominent eyes the wrinkles are very slight, especially if the horse be fat; and in thin, skinny horses, the wrinkles will appear doubled, and it is to be able to examine these wrinkles carefully and accurately, that will lead to a correct opinion of the age. Over the lid of the eyes will be found several wrinkles in old horses, few in middle age, and only one in the young horse, (as nature calls for one wrinkle,) and at ten years old you will see two, then you will find for every age over ten, an additional wrinkle up to thirty years old. With practice and care, this method will be found very useful; if not always exactly correct, it will be so in the majority of cases, and even in doubtful cases it will bring you so near the exact age as to be a sufficient guide.

Dr. Mason says, that "between nine and ten years of age a horse generally loses the marks of the mouth, though there are a few exceptions, as some horses retain good mouths until they are fourteen or fifteen years old, with their teeth white, even and regular, and many other marks of freshness and vigor."

But when a horse grows old it may be discovered by these indications, which commonly attend old age, viz.: The gums wear away, and leave the roots of the teeth long and slender; the roots grow yellow, and often brownish; the bars of the mouth (which are always fleshy, plump and dry in a young horse, and form so many distinct, firm ridges,) in an old horse are lean, smooth and covered with saliva, with few or no ridges.

The eyes of a young horse appear plump, full and lively; the lids with few wrinkles, the hollows above the ball small, and no gray hairs upon the brow, unless they proceed from color or marks of the horse. The eyes of an old horse appear sleepy, dim, and sunk, and the lids loose and very much wrinkled or shriveled, with large hollows and the brow gray. The countenance of a young horse is bold, gay and lively; while that of an old one is sad, dejected and melancholy, unless mounted, and artificial means are used to give him spirit.

The chin of a horse, in my opinion, is by far the best mark to enable you to ascertain his age, inasmuch as it does not admit of the practice of those arts by which the jockey so often passes off an old broken-down horse for a young one. The appearance can be changed only by nature; and an attentive observer will soon be convinced that it is not more difficult to tell an old horse from a young one by the appearance of their chins, than it is for a skillful physician to distinguish a cheek of health from one that is wasted, diseased, and superannuated.

The chin of a young horse is round, full, plump, full of wrinkles, and the pores close and small; that of a horse advanced in years, flat, wrinkled, flabby, and the pores open and large. Indeed, after some experience, together with particular attention to this mark of age, there will be but little difficulty in ascertaining, with certainty, the age of a horse from three to nine years old.

I have sometimes met with travelers on the road, whom I never before had seen, and in traveling along have told the age of their horses by their chins. An examination of the lips and nostrils of a horse may aid, corroborate, and strengthen the opinion of age, founded on the appearance of the chin. The lips and nostrils of a young horse are smooth and free from wrinkles, while those of an old horse abound with them.

The physiognomy of a horse will assist much in ascertaining his age; but the chin is certainly the safest guide.

I will here introduce, for the benefit of the reader, an extract from the "*American Farmer*," referring to an idea of Dr. Mason's. Dr. Mason in his work refers to the same extract in the "*American Farmer*," which I here quote:

"Since the age of that noble animal, the horse, after a certain period of life (that is, after the marks in his *incisors* and *cuspidati* are so entirely obliterated as to give no clue for ascertaining his age,) appears to the generality of *horse age judges* to be a subject of very much uncertainty, I now take the liberty of laying before the public, through the medium of your paper, an infallible method (subject to very few exceptions) of ascertaining it in such a manner, after a horse loses his marks, or after he arrives at the age of nine years or over, so that any person concerned in horses, even of the meanest capacity, may not be imposed upon in a horse's age, from nine years of age and over, more than three years at farthest, until the animal arrives at the age of twenty, and *upwards*, by just feeling the submaxillary bone, or the bone of the lower jaw.

This method I discovered by making many anatomical observations on the skulls of dead horses, and repeated dissections. In order, therefore, to elucidate the above, I must in the first place beg leave to remark that the submaxillary bone, or the bone of the lower jaw of all young horses about four or five years of age, immediately above the *bifurcation*, is invariably thick and very round at the bottom; the cavity of said bone being very small, contains a good deal of marrow, and generally continues in this state until the animal arrives at that period which is generally termed an *aged horse*, or until the animal acquires his full size in height or thickness (or, according to sporting language, is completely furnished,) with very little variation. But after this period, the cavity as aforesaid becomes larger, and more marrow is contained therein. Hence the submaxillary bone becomes thinner and sharper a little above the *bifurcation*.

This indelible mark may always be observed in a small degree in horses above eight years of age, but at nine years old it is still more perceptible. It continues growing a little thinner and sharper at the bottom until twelve years of age. From thence until fifteen it is still thinner, and about as sharp as the back of a case-knife near the handle. From this period, until the ages eighteen, nineteen, twenty and upwards, it is exceedingly so; and is as sharp, in many subjects, as the dull edge of that instrument.

RULES.

First.—Put your three fingers about half an inch or an inch immediately above the bifurcation, and grasp the submaxillary bone, or the lower jaw. If it is thick at the sides, and very round indeed at the bottom, the animal is most certainly under nine years of age.

Second.—If the bone is not very thick, and it is perceivably not very round at the bottom, he is from nine to twelve years old, and so on. From twelve to fifteen, the bone is sharper at bottom and thinner at the sides, the bottom is generally as sharp as the back of a case-knife; and from fifteen to eighteen, nineteen, twenty and upwards, without any exceptions, the bone, when divested of its integuments, is as sharp as the dull edge of that instrument.

Third.—Allowances must always be made between heavy, large western or wagon horses, or carriage horses, and fine blooded ones. By practicing and strictly attending to these rules, upon all descriptions of horses, the performer in a little time will become very accurate in the accomplishment of his desires, more especially if he attentively observes the lower jaw-bone of dead horses."

The next subject we treat of is the shape and appearance of horses that are required for different descriptions of work, such as the saddle horse, carriage horse and race horse. We have therefore placed before you the opinion of Dr Mason, who appears to have taken quite a lively interest in the subject, and from his manner of treating it, I do not think that I can do better than quote it. He says.

SADDLE HORSE.

"When a horse is purchased for the saddle alone, it is to be presumed he must be clear of all defects, strike the fancy, entirely please the eye, and, from his happy symmetry and due proportion of form, stand the second beauty in the world. When this is the case, he is seldom disposed of at too high a price. Amongst the great number of people in the United States, I am induced to believe there are but few good judges of a horse calculated for the saddle. Indeed, they are better informed upon almost *any other* subject that can be mentioned. Yet the Virginians have a large number of fine horses, and are accused of devoting too much attention to that beautiful animal. Among all the difficulties attending the affairs of common life, there is not, perhaps, a greater than that of choosing a beautiful, an elegant, or good horse. Nor will this appear strange when we consider the number of circumstances that are to be taken into consideration, with regard to shape, size, movements, limbs, marks, eyes, color, age, etc., etc., which are so various that it would fill a volume to describe; and, indeed, the best judges are often obliged to content themselves with guessing at some things, unless they have sufficient time to make a thorough trial. If I were asked what were the two most beautiful objects in nature, I would answer, that woman, lovely woman, before whose charms the soul of man bows with reverence and submission, stands

SADDLE HORSE.

unparalleled; next to this matchless paragon, a beautiful horse displays nature in her highest polish and greatest perfection; his gay and cheerful appearance, proudly prancing and bounding, his elegance of shape, smoothness of limbs, polish of skin, due proportion of form, and gracefulness of action, united to a mild, soft, faithful and patient disposition, raise him far above the rest of the brute creation.

I shall now proceed to lay down some rules, and to give some hints for the guidance of persons requiring a saddle horse.

In order that he may have just claim to beauty and elegance, his head must be small, thin, bony and tapering; his countenance lively and cheerful; his ears quick in action, high, erect, narrow, thin, and pointing together; his eyes large, round, full and black, sparkling with cheerfulness, yet hushing his agitating passions into order and obedience; his nostrils large and expanded, and, when in motion, disclosing a deep red color; his brows and forehead smooth, and not too flat; his nose somewhat rising, of good turn, and a little inclined to the Roman shape; his neck long, thin, delicate and arched, forming a beautiful gradation from the breast and shoulders; his mane half the width of his neck, thin and smooth; his shoulders high, tapering, and thrown well back; his breast plump, full, and of moderate width· his fore-legs straight, flat, sinewy and thin; his arms large and muscular; his back not too short, and not too much swayed for strength and durability, but pretty even and straight; his body rather round and swelling than flat, and of proportionable size; his flanks plump and full, and the last rib approaching near the hip bones; his hips and buttocks full, round and well covered with muscles; his chine broad; his tail well placed, and naturally or artificially elegant, which adds much to his figure and gay appearance; his thighs long, from the hip to the haunch-bone large and bulging with muscles; his hocks broad, sinewy, bony, and clear of puffs; his hind-legs from the hocks short, bending a little rather than straight, flat and sinewy; his pasterns of moderate length, small and bony; his hoofs cupped;* small, round and smooth; his hind-parts not tucked, but of easy turn and graceful slope; when mounted his appearance should be bold, lofty, majestic; his eyes shining with intrepidity and fire; his movements light and airy as a phantom, with a fairy step that would scarcely break a dew-drop; his action smooth and graceful; his color should suit the taste of the purchaser, though a mahogany bay is certainly the best color; his marks large, of irregular white, to light up the countenance, and at least two white legs, which will add much to his beauty, though it must be acknowledged that all parts of a horse that are white, are much more tender than any other color.

When a horse is ridden by any person for you to judge of his gaits, you should have him moved towards you, from you, and finally by you, as you may have the opportunity of discovering if there is any turning in and out about his knees and ankles, before or behind, which is very objectionable. A well shaped horse will track as true (or his legs will follow each other in as direct a line) as the wheels of a well constructed carriage. For him to be considered a good riding horse, he should move with ease to himself, and pass over the ground with great rapidity. Hard steps, short going, and great apparent labor, are offensive to the sight, unpleasant to the rider, and fatiguing to the horse himself.

* I think that the hoof only requires to be very slightly cupped.—Ed.

With respect to the colors of horses, people differ very widely; a black horse, with white face and legs, a gray, or a mahogany bay, with white marks, when well kept, are all showy colors; but for actual service, experience has proved that dark colors, without any white feet, are far preferable; for who ever recollects to have seen a black, sorrel, or bay horse, with a bald face and four white legs, distinguish himself on the turf, in four-mile heats? I am inclined to believe there is no first rate race horse of that description within the United States."

CARRIAGE HORSES.

"Horses intended for a carrage or draft of any description should be from five feet to five feet four inches high; though there are many excellent and truly valuable draft horses of much smaller size. The greatest attention should be paid to their habits, temper, quality and disposition. A horse that has been once frightened in harness, never again is safe for that employment. So retentive are their memories, that they do not forget an alarm of that kind during their whole lives. For the want of experience on this subject, horses that have been frightened in harness have been hitched to carriages, which too often has been the cause of the untimely death of many amiable females and helpless children. Indeed, a pair of good and well-matched gentle carriage horses is rarely to be met with; as so many good qualities, together with a similarity of age, color, size, and marks are required to make them complete and valuable. Their eyes should be good, carriage lofty, bodies proportionably large, breast full and wide, their whole bodies heavily muscled; their heads, necks, and ears delicate; their legs large, sinewy, and bony; their pasterns short, and their hoofs moderately large, and not too flat. They should be free from starting, stumbling, and kicking, and their dispositions patient, gentle, and obedient. It very often happens that horses are kept together as a match, on account of their color and similarity of marks, when no respect is paid to their difference of form, spirit, and movements, which often differ as widely as the mettled racer from the dull cart horse. When thus badly matched, they would very soon be separated by a *good judge*, and nothing short of necessity should ever permit them to draw together. Carriage horses should carry good tails, naturally, or artificially,* which adds much to their gay and elegant appearance; presenting figures ready, apparently, to move upon the wind, whilst they are perfectly gentle and manageable. Horses of different colors, whose spirit, size, and movements are similar, are a much better match in harness than those of the same color with three or four inches difference in height; or one dull and the other spirited; one young, the other old; one fat, the other poor; one with a bald face and white legs, the other with white legs; or one active and the other clumsy.

I have thus taken up the time of the reader, to make him the better judge, and give him a correct idea of a bad match of carriage horses, which will assist him much in selecting those that are good. After being thoroughly satisfied about the shape, age, condition, &c., of a pair of carriage horses you may be about to purchase, it will be necessary, in justice to yourself, to try them in harness; though the seller will assure you they are as gentle as lambs, true as honor, and finally, the best pair of horses in the world; although it is possible for such a statement to be a

* The plan of nicking, to satisfy the fancy of their owners, we disapprove of on principle, as it is both cruel and brutal, and should never be allowed by Mr. Bergh's Society.—Ed.

fact, I would advise that a trial should be made, and the purchaser become his own judge; for which purpose have them hitched to a carriage, and driven several times up and down the steepest hill that the road may cross, which is most convenient. If they have any tricks, or are not true draft horses, it can be readily discovered. Next, for the purpose of discovering if they have ever been alarmed in harness, frequently open and shut the carriage door, also move and rattle the steps. If they have ever been frightened in harness you will very soon be compelled to desist; then by coming to their front, and with attention observing their ears and eyes, you will be informed to your entire satisfaction if they are safe. Horses that have been once alarmed in harness, so soon as they hear any rattling noise behind them, begin to grow restless, sinking or squatting behind, holding the head high, snorting, fetching long breaths, moving the ears with great quickness, at the same time showing the whites of their eyes. Let me warn the reader against the purchase of such horses: they are unfit and unsafe for the use of a family.

Horses for harness, that are fiery and fretful, are very objectionable, and should always be avoided; but great care should be taken to distinguish between animals of this description and those that are eager and spirited; the former begin to prance and fret the moment they are out of the stable, until they exhaust themselves with fatigue; but the latter endeavor only to be first in the chase, or foremost in the field, and are truly valuable; possessing those qualities that resemble prudence and courage; the others, intemperate heat and rashness. Whenever carriage horses are driven, they should be moved off fifteen or twenty steps in a slow walk, without the cracking or flourishing of a whip, which is so much the custom, and which is very frequently the cause of high-tempered horses refusing to draw; after which their speed may be quickened to whatever gait you may prefer, by the use of some kind word, to which all horses should be accustomed. It is very much the practice with drivers to leave their horses standing in a carriage, without any person to hold them, for hours together. Having seen the worst of consequences result from this practice (and with horses under the character of being gentle,) I would recommend that drivers should never give up their reins until they are prepared with some person sufficiently strong to hold them. By using such precaution, the overturning and breaking of many fine carriages, and the ruining of many valuable and elegant carriage horses, would be avoided."

RACE HORSE.

"It is a remarkable fact that horses run in all shapes. But most generally those excel upon the turf, that are of the following form:—head and neck thin, small, and delicate; eyes large, plump, and full of expression; nostrils wide, red, and expanded; throttle large; shoulders high, thin, and running very far back; breast plump, full and wide; body long, round, and rather light than heavy; back short as possible; thighs long, large, full, and bulging; forearm large and swelling towards the breast; hocks broad, strong and bony; legs of moderate size, thin, flat and sinewy; pasterns rather long and small, than otherwise; feet of proportionable size to the balance of the form, though, of the two extremes, small is better; he should be nervous, tractable, and of good spirit, and he should be from five feet to five feet four inches high. Such a horse, well managed, kept and placed in races, will seldom fail to distinguish himself on the turf."

"It may be generally remarked, that men who drive fast have swift horses; not that they drive fast because they have swift horses, but because fast driving makes horses swift. A horse may commonly be trained to a dull and heavy, or to an airy and fleet gait. Nature unquestionably does much, but education does far more towards producing the great difference in the speed of horses, than most men are willing to allow. Horses are more frequently injured by driving them beyond their *habitual* pace, than beyond their *native* power.

The best direction for the education of horses is *drive fast, and stop often.*"

ON FEEDING, AND THE FOOD.

In adapting the quantity and quality of food to the wants of each horse, regard must be paid *first* of all to the small size of this animal's stomach, which affects all alike; *secondly*, to the work for which he is designed; and *thirdly*, to the peculiar constitution of each horse. From the first of these causes the horse must never be allowed to fast for any long period if it can be possibly avoided, it being found from experience that at the end of four hours his stomach is empty, and the whole frame becomes exhausted, while the appetite is frequently so impaired if he is kept fasting for a longer period, that when food is presented to him it will not be taken. From actual experience it has been shown that on a long journey, without a chance to feed the animal, it exhausted him less to ride fast, and increase the pace up to ten or even twelve miles an hour, and thus reduce the time of fasting, than to dawdle over the ground for a much longer time on an empty stomach. If two horses are driven or ridden fifty or sixty miles under similar conditions as to the weight they have to draw or carry, and the one is taken at the rate of six miles an hour, which will keep him fasting from eight and a half to ten hours, according to the distance, while the other is traveled fast enough to do it in six or seven hours, the latter will be less exhausted than the former, though even he would be all the better for a feed in the middle of the journey, the time devoted to this act being easily picked up by the increased energy which would be given in the corn.

The human stomach will bear hunger far better than that of the horse, and if the rider or driver feels his appetite pretty keen, he may be satisfied that the animal which carries him is still more in want of food. The kind of work which the horse is intended for, affects not only the quantity of food required, but also its quality. Thus, very fast work, such as racing and hunting, strains the muscular system, as well as the heart and lungs, to the utmost, and therefore the food which is best fitted for the development of the former to the highest degree, should consist of those kinds which present the elements contained in the muscular tissue in the largest proportions consistent with due performance of the digestive organs. Modern researches in organic chemistry have thrown considerable light on the subject of digestion. It is now ascertained beyond doubt that food consists of two characteristic elements, one being for the nourishment of the body, while the other contributes to the support of combustion in the lungs. The former contains nitrogen, the latter does not. Thus, flesh, grain, and pulse contain nitrogen, and are capable of affording nourishment, while oil, fat, and starch, are only able to supply carbon for the purpose of respiration and nutrition to the non-nitrogenous parts. These are found in *Black Butter-Corn* in larger proportion than in any other description of food, as one pint of Butter-Corn is considered equal to twelve quarts of oats. Butter-Corn has recently been imported into this country from the Indies, and can be found at many of the feed stores. The demands of the muscular system are fully supplied by the Black Butter-Corn, as it contains more saline matter than hay, more albumen, starch, fibrine, and sugar, than oats or Indian corn, and more fatty matter than linseed or slippery elm; and, on the other hand, contains less woody fibre, which is the waste of food.

A feed of one pint of the Black Butter-Corn per day will be more nourishing to a horse than a peck of oats, as it not only fattens, but, from the quantity of its fatty matter, it is as cooling as linseed.

In the following pages, therefore, I shall give a description of the several alimentary wants of the horse, and then show in what proportions they are found in the varieties of keep, which have in a measure been described, so as to enable the horse master to make his selection according to circumstances. All these substances are found in the blood, but this fluid is continually receiving and giving off its various elements. The blood of a horse fed on highly nitrogenized food does not differ on analysis from that of another which has been kept on the opposite kind of diet. Physiological research, however, tells us that muscle is chiefly composed of fibrine, and that every time a bundle of its fibres contracts, a certain expenditure of this material is made, calling for a corresponding supply from the blood, which cannot be offered unless the food contains it. Hence the badly-fed horse, if worked, soon loses his flesh, and not only becomes free from fat, but also presents a contracted condition of the muscles, and thus science is confirmed by every-day experience, and the fact is generally admitted that to increase the muscular powers of a horse he must have a sufficient supply of nitrogenized food. As I have before remarked, the nutrition of muscle requires fibrine; but, in addition, the brain and nerves must be supplied with fatty matter, phosphorus, and albumen. The bones demand gelatin and earthy salts, and the maintenance of heat cannot be effected without carbon in some shape or other.

It may therefore be taken for granted that the much-worked horse requires oats, and most of all, *Black Butter-Corn*, or a mixed feed of oats and the Butter-Corn, together with such an amount of hay as will supply him with the starch and gum which his system requires; while, on the other hand, for the idle or light-used animal, which does not use his muscular system to any extent, and therefore does not require much oats or hay, a much less quantity of feed, with a pint of Black Butter-Corn three or four times a week, would do more to improve the health and condition of the animal than all the swindling preparations, under the term of *condition powders*, which, in nine cases out of ten, are more hurtful than beneficial; but there is no doubt that there are many persons who can be made to believe anything, and it is only by that class that these preparations are thought much of. Not that alterative medicines are not beneficial at the proper time, but the compounds made generally under that term are such stuff, that it is next to an impossibility for any benefit to be got out of them. The Black Butter-Corn being the finest feed now in the country, I think that I should be acting injustly to my readers if I did not acquaint them of it, and demonstrate clearly why I so advocate it; and this is best done by an analysis of its alimentary elements.

The following table exhibits the percentage of these various elements in the several kinds of food for the horse, most frequently used in this, as well as other countries:

Description of Food.	Woody Fibre.	Sugar and Starch.	Fibrine and Albumen	Fatty Matter.	Saline Matters	Water.
Black Butter-Corn..	none.	53.5	15.5	10.5	9.2	11.3
Oats	30.0	43.0	11.4	0.6	2.5	12.5
Indian Corn	8.0	53.0	14.0	6.0	5.0	14.0
Linseed	19.0	35.0	20.0	8.0	6.0	12.0
Beans	14.5	40.0	26.0	2.5	3.0	14.0
Peas	9.0	48.0	24.0	2.0	3.0	14.0
Barley	14.0	52.0	13.5	2.5	3.0	15.0
Old Hay	30.0	40.0	7.0	2.0	7.0	14.0
Clover	25.0	40.0	9.0	3.0	9.0	14.0
Barley Straw	46.0	34.0	1.5	none.	6.5	12.0
Oat Straw	50.0	31.0	1.0	a trace	5.5	12.5
Wheat Straw.	55.0	27.0	0.5	none.	5.5	12.0
Bran	54.0	2.0	20.0	4.0	7.0	13.0
Carrots	3.0	10.0	1.5	none.	1.5	84.0

From this table it will be seen that the black butter-corn must be the best feed, then corn and oats, with hay.

The best mode of feeding hard-worked horses is as follows:

AT NIGHT, AFTER WORK—One quarter-peck oats, and one half-pint black butter-corn, with eight to ten pounds of hay, cut or otherwise.

IN THE MORNING—One quarter-peck oats, and one pint Indian meal, with a little hay, say two pounds.

DURING THE DAY—One quarter-peck of oats.

ON SATURDAY NIGHT—A good warm bran mash.

ON SUNDAY—An extra allowance of hay.

By following these rules, the food which a horse consumes during one week will be found to contain as follows:

Fibrine and albumen, 22 lbs.; Fat, 5½ lbs.; Starch and sugar, 85 lbs.

So that the relative proportion of nitrogenous to carbonaceous food is as 1 to 4; whilst for a fattening animal it is as 1 to 5.

Let the animal in all cases have his water before feeding him.

A TABLE

OF THE

BONES IN THE STRUCTURE OF THE HORSE.

From Dr. Dadd's "Anatomy and Physiology."

BONES OF THE HEAD

Bones of the cranium or skull:
- Frontal 1
- Parietal 2
- Occipital 1
- Temporal 2
- Ethmoid 1
- Sphenoid 1

Bones of the face:
- Nasal 2
- Ungius 2
- Malarum 2
- Maxillaria, superior and anterior ... 4
- Palatine 2
- Turbinated bones 4
- Vomer 1
- Posterior maxilla 1
- Lachrymal 2

Dentes, or teeth:
- Cuspidata, or canine 4
- Molars 24
- Incisors 12

Bone of the tongue:
- Hyoides 1

Bones of the ear:
- Malleus 2
- Incus 2
- Stapes 2
- Orbicular 2

BONES OF TRUNK

Spine — Vertebræ:
- Cervical 7
- Dorsal 18
- Lumbar 5
- Sacrum .. * 1

Tail—ossa coccygis, or bones of the tail 15

Thorax:
- Sternum, composed at birth of a number of pieces 1
- True ribs 14
- False ribs 22

Pelvis, ossa innominata† 2

Carried forward 162

---

* The bones in the sacrum of the colt consist of five pieces.

† The pelvis of the young animal is made up of the two ossa innominata, each of which is formed of two pieces; the larger is called os ileum, the smaller, in allusion to the human pelvis, has been subdivided into two portions, named os ischium and os pubis.

NUMBER OF BONES IN A HORSE.

		Brought forward...............	162
BONES OF THE FORE EXTREMITIES.	Shoulder...........	Scapula	2
	Arm...............	Humerus.................	2
	Fore-arm...........	Radius (and Ulna, connected with the former)...........	4
	Bones of the knee....	Os schapoides, (1 to each knee)	2
		Os lunare...... " "	2
		Os cuneiforme.. " "	2
		Os trapezium... " "	2
		Os trapezoides.. " "	2
		Os unciforme... " "	2
		Os magnum.... " "	2
		Os pisiforme... " "	2
	Below the knee	Metacarpus magnus..........	2
		Splents.....................	4
		Sessamoides	4
		Suffraginis (large pastern).....	2
		Os coronæ (small pastern).....	2
		Os naviculare................	2
		Os pedis	2
BONES OF THE HIND EXTREMITIES.	Thigh...............	Femur......................	2
	Stifle..............	Patella	2
	Leg................	Tibia......................	2
		Fibula.....................	2
	Bones of the hock....	Astragalus..................	2
		Os calcis...................	2
		Os cuboides.................	2
		Os cuneiforme magnum.......	2
		Internal medium.............	2
		External medium.............	2
	Below the knee.......	Metatarsi (or canons).........	2
		Splents.....................	4
		Os suffraginis...............	2
		Os coronæ..................	2
		Os sesamoidis...............	4
		Os naviculare...............	2
		Os pedis....................	2
		Total........................	242

Dr. Hooper reckons the number of bones in the human subject at 248.

DICK & FITZGERALD,
PUBLISHERS, NEW YORK.

⁎ The Publishers, upon receipt of the price, will send any of the following books by mail, POSTAGE FREE, to any part of the United States. In ordering books, the full name, post office, county and State should be plainly written.

Dick's Encyclopedia of Practical Receipts and Processes. Containing over 6,400 Receipts; embracing thorough information, in plain language, applicable to almost every possible industrial and domestic requirement. The scope of this work is different from any other book of the kind. The contents of the Encyclopedia are collated from works on the various subjects by authors of eminence in their respective branches, divested of technicalites, simplified and illustrated by diagrams, where necessary, so as to make the whole plain and intelligible to the uninitiated. This work presents a complete and indispensable book for the household, farm, garden, &c.; including instructions as to what to do and how to do it, in case of all accidents, contingencies, and ailments of daily life. It also affords a valuable Book of Reference for the Druggist, enabling him to make up a number of "Sundries," especially Toilet Soaps, Dentifrices, Cosmetics, and Perfumery; also specific Medicines and Remedies derived from the practice of eminent Physicians, or from various European officinal sources; thus forming a useful and desirable adjunct to the United States Pharmacopœia. It enables the Grocer to prepare his own Flavoring Extracts, Vinegar, and a host of other articles, cheaper and better than he can purchase them; and to test the quality of some of the Goods that he buys and sells. To the Liquor Dealer it gives the best and latest methods of treating and improving his liquors; of preparing Cordials, &c.; of making, managing, and bottling all kinds of Wines, Cider, &c.,—it lays before the workman the results obtained by the experiments and experience of the masters of his trade. In fact it is almost useless to attempt an enumeration of the advantages of this work, as there is scarcely a branch of Industry that may not derive information and profit from its pages. The Index of this work occupies 42 three-column pages, in small type. 600 pages, royal octavo, cloth.
Price..$5.00.
Bound in half calf, extra...$7.50.
☞ Full descriptive circular of the above sent, by mail, free.

The Parlor Stage. A Collection of Drawing-room Proverbs, Charades and Tableaux Vivants. By Miss S. A. Frost. The authoress of this attractive volume has performed her task with skill, talent, and we might say, with genius; for the Acting Charades and Proverbs are really minor dramas of a high order of merit. There are twenty-four of them, and fourteen *Tableaux*, all of which are excellent. The characters are admirably drawn, well contrasted, and the plots and dialogues deeply interesting. 358 pages, small 8vo, cloth, gilt side and back, beveled edges. Price **$1.50**

Wilson's Book of Recitations and Dialogues. With Instructions in Elocution and Declamation. Containing a choice selection of Poetical and Prose Recitations and Original Colloquies. Designed as a Reading Book for Classes, and as an Assistant to Teachers and Students in preparing Exhibitions. By Floyd B. Wilson, Professor of Elocution. The Colloquies are entirely original. Paper covers. Price...............30 cts.
Bound in boards, cloth back..50 cts.

Popular Books sent Free of Postage at the Prices annexed.

The Parlor Magician; or, One Hundred Tricks for the Drawing-Room,
containing an Extensive and Miscellaneous Collection of Conjuring and Legerdemain; Sleights with Dice, Dominoes, Cards, Ribbons, Rings, Fruit, Coin, Balls, Handkerchiefs, etc., all of which may be performed in the Parlor or Drawing-Room, without the aid of any apparatus; also embracing a choice variety of Curious Deceptions, which may be performed with the aid of simple apparatus; the whole illustrated and clearly explained with 121 engravings. Paper Covers. Price................30 cts.
Bound in boards, with cloth back..50 cts.

Book of Riddles and Five Hundred Home Amusements.
Containing a Choice and Curious Collection of Riddles, Charades, Enigmas, Rebuses, Anagrams, Transpositions, Conundrums, Amusing Puzzles, Queer Sleights, Recreations in Arithmetic, Fireside Games and Natural Magic, embracing Entertaining Amusements in Magnetism, Chemistry, Second Sight and Simple Recreations in Science for Family and Social Pastime, illustrated with sixty Engravings. Paper covers. Price..............30 cts.
Bound in boards, with cloth back...50 cts.

Book of Fireside Games.
Containing an Explanation of the most Entertaining Games suited to the Family Circle as a Recreation, such as Games of Action, Games which merely require attention, Games which require memory, Catch Games, which have for their objects Tricks or Mystification, Games in which an opportunity is afforded to display Gallantry, Wit, or some slight knowledge of certain Sciences, Amusing Forfeits, Fireside Games for Winter Evening Amusement, etc.
Paper covers. Price..30 cts.
Bound in boards, with cloth back...50 cts.

Parlor Theatricals; or, Winter Evenings' Entertainment.
Containing Acting Proverbs. Dramatic Charades, Acting Charades, or Drawing-Room Pantomimes, Musical Burlesques, Tableaux Vivants, etc.; with Instructions for Amateurs; how to Construct a Stage and Curtain; how to get up Costumes and Properties; on the "Making up" of Characters; Exits and Entrances; how to arrange Tableaux, etc. Illustrated with Engravings. Paper covers. Price......................................30 cts.
Bound in boards, cloth back...50 cts.

The Book of 500 Curious Puzzles.
Containing a large collection of entertaining Paradoxes, Perplexing Deceptions in numbers, and Amusing Tricks in Geometry. By the author of "The Sociable," "The Secret Out," "The Magician's Own Book." Illustrated with a great variety of Engravings. This book commands a large sale. It will furnish fun and amusement for a whole winter. Paper covers. Price..............30 cts.
Bound in boards, with cloth back...50 cts.

The above five books are compiled from the "Sociable" and "Magician's Own."

The American Boys' Book of Sports and Games.
A Repository of In and Out-Door Amusements for Boys and Youth. Illustrated with nearly 700 engravings, designed by White, Herrick, Weir and Harvey, and engraved by N. Orr. This is, unquestionably, the most attractive and valuable book of its kind ever issued in this or any other country. It has been three years in preparation, and embraces all the sports and games that tend to develop the physical constitution, improve the mind and heart, and relieve the tedium of leisure hours, both in the parlor and the field. The Engravings are all in the finest style of art, and embrace eight full-page ornamental titles, illustrating the several departments of the work, beautifully printed on tinted paper. The book is issued in the best style, being printed on fine sized paper, and handsomely bound. Extra cloth, gilt side and back, extra gold. Price...$3 50
Extra cloth, full gilt edges, back and side.......................................$4 00

Popular Books sent Free of Postage at the Prices annexed.

McBride's All Kinds of Dialogues. A Collection of Original Humorous and Domestic Dialogues, introducing Yankee, French, Irish, Dutch, and other characters. Excellently adapted for Amateur performance. By H. Elliott McBride. This book constitutes a second series of McBride's Comic Dialogues, and affords an additional variety of the spirited dialogues and short dramatic scenes contained in the latter book. They are all entirely original, and develop in a marked degree the eccentricities and peculiarities of the various ideal, but genuine, characters which are represented in them. They are specially adapted for School Exhibitions and all other celebrations where the success of the entertainment is partly or entirely dependent on the efforts of the young folks.
Illuminated Paper Cover, Price .... 30 cts.
Bound in Boards .... 50 cts.

Beecher's Recitations and Readings. Humorous, Serious, Dramatic; including Prose and Poetical Selections in Dutch, French, Yankee, Irish, Backwoods, Negro and other Dialects. Edited by Alvah C. Beecher. This excellent selection has been compiled to meet a growing demand for Public Readings, and contains a number of the favorite pieces that have been rendered with telling effect by the most popular Public Readers of the present time. It includes, also, choice selections for Recitation, and is, therefore, admirably adapted for use at Evening Entertainments, School Celebrations, and other Festival occasions.
16mo. Illuminated Paper Cover, Price .... 30 cts.
Bound in Boards .... 50 cts.

Day's Cards for Popping the Question. An Original Game for Lovers and Sweethearts, or for Merry-Making in a Party of Young People. These cards are not only delightfully useful to diffident lovers—enabling them to realize deferred hopes, and cure aching hearts, but will make lots of fun and innocent amusement in a party of young people, often resulting in earnest love passages begun in sport—preventing shyness and diffidence, and promoting that healthy and easy confidence between the sexes so necessary in all social meetings. The set consists of forty-two Cards, viz.: twenty-one questions, which are mostly earnest declarations of love, and twenty-one answers, equally pithy and to the point. As soon as these Cards become known we feel sure that they will have an endless sale. Put up in cases, with directions for playing. Price .... 30 cts.

Ned Turner's Circus Joke Book. A Collection of the best Jokes, Bon Mots, Repartees, Gems of Wit, and Funny Sayings and Doings of the celebrated Equestrian Clown and Ethiopian Comedian, Ned Turner. Arranged and compiled by George E. Gowan. This book forms the third of the series by this versatile popular performer. Price .... 10 cts.

Chips from Uncle Sam's Jack-Knife. Illustrated with over 100 Comical Engravings, and comprising a collection of over 500 Laughable Stories, Funny Adventures, Comic Poetry, Queer Conundrums, Terrific Puns, Witty Sayings, Sublime Jokes and Sentimental Sentences. The whole being a most perfect portfolio for those who love to laugh.
Large octavo. Price .... 25 cts.

Clarence Bolton. A New York story, with city life in all its phases. This is one of those fascinating tales of city life that gives an insight into every class of society. Price .... 25 cts.

Grace Weldon; or, *The Pretty Milliner.* This is a story about the Sewing Girls of Boston. Full of fun and adventure. Any person who desires to read a lively story should not fail to get this work.
Price .... 25 cts.

Popular Books sent Free of Postage at the Prices annexed.

Delisser's Horseman's Guide. Comprising the Laws on Warranty, and the Rules in purchasing and selling Horses, with the decisions and reports of various courts in Europe and the United States; to which is added a detailed account of what constitute soundness and unsoundness, and a precise method. simply laid down, for the examination of horses, showing their age to thirty years old; together with an exposure of the various tricks and impositions practiced by low horse-dealers (jockeys) on inexperienced persons; also a valuable Table of each and every bone in the structure of the Horse. The entire matter carefully compiled from Twenty English, Five American, Six French, and Nine German Veterinary Authors, with the opinions of the compiler attached. By George P. Delisser, V. S. & L. A., and late Examining Veterinary Surgeon to the American Society for the Prevention of Cruelty to Animals. Bound in boards, cloth back.... **75 cts.** Bound in Cloth. Price..**$1.00.**

Howard's Book of Conundrums and Riddles. Containing over 1,400 Witty Conundrums, Queer Riddles, Perplexing Puzzles, Ingenious Enigmas, Clever Charades, Curious Catches, and Amusing Sells. original and newly dressed. This splendid collection of curious paradoxes will afford the material for a never-ending feast of fun and amusement. Any person, with the assistance of this book, may take the lead in entertaining a company and keeping them in roars of laughter for hours together. It is an invaluable companion for a Pic-nic or Summer Excursion of any kind, and is just the thing to make a fireside circle merry on a long winter's evening. There is not a poor riddle in the book, the majority being fresh and of the highest order. Paper cover. Price...............**30 cts.** Bound in boards, cloth back. Price............................**50 cts.**

Frost's Book of Tableaux and Shadow Pantomimes. Containing a choice collection of Tableaux or living Pictures, embracing Moving Tableaux, Mother Goose Tableaux, Fairy Tale Tableaux. Charade and Proverb Tableaux; together with directions for arranging the stage, costuming the characters, and forming appropriate groups. By Miss S. Annie Frost. To which is added a number of Shadow Acts and Pantomines, with complete stage instructions. 180 pages, paper cover...**30 cts.** Bound in boards, cloth back......................................**50 cts.**

Laughing Gas. An Encyclopædia of Wit, Wisdom, and Wind. By Sam Slick, Jr. Comically illustrated with 100 original and laughable Engravings, and nearly 500 side-extending Jokes, and other things to get fat on; and the best thing of it is, that everything about the book is new and fresh—all new—new designs, new stories, new type—no comic almanac stuff. Price...**25 cts.**

The Egyptian Dream Book and Fortune-Teller. Containing an Alphabetical List of Dreams, and numerous methods of Telling Fortunes, including the celebrated Oraculum of Napoleon Bonaparte. Illustrated with explanatory diagrams. Boards, cloth back. Price...**40 cts.**

Ned Turner's Black Jokes. A collection of Funny Stories, Jokes and Conundrums, interspersed with Witty Sayings and Humorous Dialogues. As given by Ned Turner, the Celebrated Ethiopian Delineator and Equestrian Clown. Price..**10 cts.**

Ned Turner's Clown Joke Book. Containing the best Jokes and Gems of Wit, composed and delivered by the favorite Equestrian Clown and Ethiopian Comedian, Ned Turner. 18mo. Price...............**10 cts.**

Sam Slick in Search of a Wife. 12mo. Paper cover. Price...**75 cts.**

Popular Books sent Free of Postage at the Prices Annexed.

Cards of Courtship. Arranged with such apt Conversations that you will be enabled to ask the momentous question categorically, in such a delicate manner that the girl will not suspect what you are at. These cards may be used, either by two persons, or they will make lots of fun for an evening party of young people. There are fourteen question cards, and twenty-eight answers—forty-two in all. Each answer will respond differently to every one of the questions. The person holding the questions either selects or draws one out, as he pleases. The answer is given by shuffling the answer cards, and then throwing one of them down promiscuously. It may be a warm and loving, a non-committal, a genial assenting, a cold denying, an evasive, or even a coquettishly uncertain answer, —for they are all there, besides others which it is difficult to classify. When used in a party, the question is read aloud by the lady receiving it—she shuffles and hands out an answer—and that also must be read aloud by the gentleman receiving it. The fun thus caused is intense. Put up in handsome card cases, on which are printed directions. Price........30 cts.

Love-Making Made Easy. By Love-Letter Cards. We have just printed a new and novel Set of Cards which will delight the hearts of young people susceptible of the tender passion. These consist of forty-two cards—twenty-one pink, or yellow, and the same number of white ones. Each white card has printed on it a love-letter to a lady, and each of the colored ones has her reply. The letters and replies are all different, and no formality of style, or namby-pambyism, will be found in any of them. All are written in a modern familiar tone, with plain and candid declarations of love--warmly or moderately expressed, or delicately hinted at, as the case may be, and some of them boldly popping the momentous question to the fair recipient. The answer cards are equally terse, candid and to the point. N. B.—These cards may be also successfully used for models (either wholly or in part) in writing to lovers or sweethearts. Put up in handsome cases on which are printed directions. Price..............................30 cts.

Fortune-Telling Cards. Solutions of uncertain and intricate questions relative to love, luck, lotteries, matrimony, business matters, journeys, and future events generally, are here given in a direct, piquant, and satisfactory manner. They have been carefully worked out on genuine astrological and geometrical principles, by planetarium, and in figures, triangles and curves, and are so arranged that each answer will respond to every one of the questions which may be put. There are fourteen printed questions and twenty-eight answer cards. If none of the questions should suit your case, you can ask any other you please, and the proper answer will come. These cards will also afford a fund of amusement in a party of young people. Each package is enclosed in a card-case, on which are printed directions for using the cards. Price...30 cts.

Leap-Year Cards. To enable any lady to pop the question to the chosen one of her heart. This set of cards is intended more to make fun among young people than for any practical utility. There are twenty-one pink or yellow cards, and the same number of white ones—forty-two in all. On each of the colored cards is a printed letter from a lady to a gentleman, wherein the fair one declares her love, or pops the question in a humorously sentimental manner. The letters all differ in style, and in the mode of attack. The twenty-one answers, on white cards, is where the fun comes in. Put up in handsome cases, on which are printed directions...........30 cts.

Souillard's Book of Practical Receipts. For the use of Families, Druggists, Perfumers, Confectioners, Patent Medicine Factors, and Dealers in Soaps and Fancy Articles for the Toilet. Compiled with great care from receipts now in use by the most popular houses in France and the United States. By F. A. Souillard, practical chemist. Paper cover. Price..25 cts.

Popular Books sent Free of Postage at the Prices annexed.

Brudder Bones' Book of Stump Speeches and Burlesque Orations.
Also containing Humorous Lectures, Ethiopian Dialogues, Plantation Scenes, Negro Farces and Burlesques, Laughable Interludes and Comic Recitations, interspersed with Dutch, Irish, French and Yankee Stories. Compiled and edited by JOHN F. SCOTT. This book contains some of the best hits of the leading negro delineators of the present time, as well as mirth-provoking jokes and repartees of the most celebrated End-Men of the day, and specially designed for the introduction of fun in an evening's entertainment. Paper covers. Price...30 cts.
Bound in boards, illuminated..50 cts.

Frost's Original Letter-Writer.
A complete collection of Original Letters and Notes, upon every imaginable subject of Every-Day Life, with plain directions about everything connected with writing a letter. Containing Letters of Introduction, Letters on Business, Letters answering Advertisements, Letters of Recommendation, Applications for Employment, Letters of Congratulation, of Condolence, of Friendship and Relationship, Love Letters, Notes of Invitation, Notes Accompanying Gifts, Letters of Favor, of Advice, and Letters of Excuse, together with an appropriate answer to each. The whole embracing three hundred letters and notes. By S. A. FROST, author of "The Parlor Stage," "Dialogues for Young Folks," etc. To which is added a comprehensive Table of Synonyms alone worth double the price asked for the book. This work is not a rehash of English writers, but is entirely practical and original, and suited to the wants of the American public. We assure our readers that it is the best collection of letters ever published in this country. Bound in boards, cloth back, with illuminated sides. Price..50 cts.

Inquire Within *for Anything you Want to Know; or, Over* 3,700 *Facts for the People.*
"Inquire Within" is one of the most valuable and extraordinary volumes ever presented to the American public, and embodies nearly 4,000 facts, in most of which any person will find instruction, aid and entertainment. It contains so many valuable recipes, that an enumeration of them requires *seventy-two columns of fine type for the index*. Illustrated. 436 large pages. Price.....................$1 50

The Sociable; *or, One Thousand and One Home Amusements.*
Containing Acting Proverbs, Dramatic Charades, Acting Charades, Tableaux Vivants, Parlor Games and Parlor Magic, and a choice collection of Puzzles, etc., illustrated with nearly 300 Engravings and Diagrams, the whole being a fund of never-ending entertainment. By the author of the "Magician's Own Book." Nearly 400 pages, 12 mo. cloth, gilt side stamp. Price..$1 50

Martine's Hand-Book of Etiquette and Guide to True Politeness.
A complete Manual for all those who desire to understand good breeding, the customs of good society, and to avoid incorrect and vulgar habits. Containing clear and comprehensive directions for correct manners, conversation, dress, introductions, rules for good behavior at Dinner Parties and the table, with hints on wine and carving at the table; together with Etiquette of the Ball and Assembly Room, Evening Parties, and the usages to be observed when visiting or receiving calls; deportment in the street and when travelling. To which is added the Etiquette of Courtship and Marriage. Bound in boards, with cloth back. Price................50 cts.
Bound in cloth, gilt side..75 cts.

Day's American Ready-Reckoner, containing Tables for
rapid calculations of Aggregate Values, Wages, Salaries, Board, Interest Money, &c., &c. Also, Tables of Timber, Plank, Board and Log Measurements, with full explanations how to measure them, either by the square foot (board measure), cubic foot (timber measure), &c. Bound in boards. Price...50 cts.
Bound in cloth...75 cts.

www.ingramcontent.com/pod-product-compliance
Lightning Source LLC
Chambersburg PA
CBHW032238080426
42735CB00008B/906